Go Figure!

Princeton Theological Monograph Series

K. C. Hanson and Charles M. Collier, Series Editors

Recent volumes in the series:

Bonnie L. Pattison
Poverty in the Theology of John Calvin

Anette Ejsing
A Theology of Anticipation: A Constructive Study of C. S. Peirce

Michael G. Cartwright
Practices, Politics, and Performance:
Toward a Communal Hermeneutic for Christian Ethics

Stephen Finlan and Vladimir Kharlamov, editors
Theōsis: Deification in Christian Theology

David A. Ackerman
Lo, I Tell You a Mystery:
Cross, Resurrection, and Paraenesis in the Rhetoric of 1 Corinthians

John A. Vissers
The Neo-Orthodox Theology of W. W. Bryden

Sam Hamstra, editor
The Reformed Pastor by John Williamson Nevin

Byron C. Bangert
Consenting to God and Nature:
Toward a Theocentric, Naturalistic, Theological Ethics

Richard Valantasis et al., editors
The Subjective Eye:
Essays in Honor of Margaret Miles

Caryn Riswold
Coram Deo:
Human Life in the Vision of God

Philip L. Mayo
"Those Who Call Themselves Jews":
The Church and Judaism in the Apocalypse of John

Go Figure!

Figuration in Biblical Interpretation

Edited by
STANLEY D. WALTERS

PICKWICK Publications · Eugene, Oregon

GO FIGURE!
Figuration in Biblical Interpretation

Princeton Theological Monograph Series 81

Pickwick Publications
A Division of Wipf and Stock Publishers
199 West 8th Avenue, Suite 3
Eugene, Oregon 97401

ISBN 13: 978-1-55635-579-0

Cataloging-in-Publication data:

Go Figure! : figuration in biblical interpretation / edited by Stanley D. Walters.

Princeton Theological Monograph Series 81

x + 164 p.; 23 cm.

ISBN 13: 978-1-55635-579-0
Includes bibliographical references.

1. Bible—Criticism, interpretation, etc.—History. 2. Typology (Theology)—History
of doctrines. I. Walters, Stanley D. II. Title. III. Series.

BS478 G5 2008

Contents

Contributors

KEITH BODNER is Professor of Religious Studies at Atlantic Baptist University. His education includes the BA from the University of Manitoba, the MCS from Regent College, and PhD degrees from both the University of Aberdeen and the University of Manchester. He is the author of several books on the books of Samuel, and numerous biblical studies.

CRAIG CARTER is Professor of Religious Studies, Tyndale University College. His education includes the BA (Hons.) from Mount Allison University, the MDiv from Acadia University, and the PhD from the University of St. Michael's College, Toronto. He is the author of *The Politics of the Cross: The Theology and Social Ethics of John Howard Yoder* (Brazos Press, 2001) and of *Rethinking Christ and Culture: A Post-Christendom Perspective* (Brazos Press, 2006).

EARL DAVEY is Provost and Professor of Music, Tyndale University College & Seminary. His education includes the BMus and MMus, the MA and PhD, all from the University of Toronto. His specializations include philosophical aesthetics and the history and philosophy of education.

BRAD FAUGHT is Associate Professor of History, Tyndale University College. His education includes the BA from the University of Calgary, the MSt from the University of Oxford, the MA from Queen's University, and the PhD from the University of Toronto. He is the author of *The Oxford Movement: A Thematic History of the Tractarians and Their Times* (Pennsylvania State University Press, 2003), as well as a number of articles and reviews. He was recently elected a Fellow of the Royal Historical Society.

JENNIFER HART WEED is Assistant Professor of Philosophy, Tyndale University College. Her education includes the BSc from the University of Western Ontario and the PhD from St. Louis University. She is the author of numerous papers in medieval philosophy, and was co-chair of the planning committee for the 2006 "Figured Out" conference.

NATHAN MACDONALD is Lecturer in the Old Testament at the University of St Andrews, Scotland. His education includes the MA and MPhil from Cambridge and the PhD from the University of Durham. He is the author of *Deuteronomy and the Meaning of Monotheism* and of many articles and reviews. He has recently won the John Templeton Award for Theological Promise (2007).

EPHRAIM RADNER is Professor of Historical Theology at Wycliffe College, University of Toronto. His education includes the PhD in systematic theology from Yale University. He has lately been priest of the Church of the Ascension in Pueblo, Colorado. He is the author of many books, including *Hope among the Fragments* and a commentary on Leviticus in the Brazos series (forthcoming).

CHRISTOPHER SEITZ is Professor of Biblical Interpretation at Wycliffe College, University of Toronto. His education includes the PhD in Old Testament from Yale University, and he has held tenured professorships at both Yale and St. Andrews. He is the author of fifteen books, including *Figured Out, Preaching and Teaching Isaiah,* and *Hermeneutics: Toward a New Introduction to the Prophets.*

FRANK ANTHONY SPINA is Professor of Old Testament at Seattle Pacific University, where he has taught since 1973. His education includes the BA from Greenville (Illinois) College, the MDiv from Asbury Theological Seminary, and the MA and PhD from the University of Michigan, Ann Arbor. He is the author of *The Faith of the Outsider* (Eerdmans: 2005) and of numerous articles in biblical studies.

STANLEY D. WALTERS is Professor of Religious Studies, Tyndale University College. His education includes the BA from Greenville (Illinois) College, the BD from Asbury Theological Seminary, the ThM from Princeton Theological Seminary, and the PhD from Yale University. He is the author of *Water for Larsa* (Yale Near Eastern Studies 4), and of numerous articles in biblical and near eastern studies.

Foreword

Earl Davey

ONCE UNDERSTOOD AS THE PRIVILEGED GROUND OF BIBLICAL SCHOL-
ars, hermeneutics is an essential aspect of a broad range of disciplines. In
the first decade of the nineteenth century, Schleiermacher, a Protestant
theologian and philosopher, extended the reach of hermeneutics to non-
biblical texts and linguistic utterances. In the latter part of the nineteenth
century, Wilhelm Dilthey began to apply hermeneutics to the human
sciences, particularly in the fields of cultural and social history. Several decades later, Martin Heidegger applied hermeneutics to philosophical and
poetical texts. Since the work of Ricoeur, Gadamer, Derrida and others in
the 1960s, hermeneutics is now an intellectual discipline in its own right,
replete with its characteristic philosophical challenges. It continues to have
cross-disciplinary application.

Accordingly, it is not surprising that the conference entitled "Figured
Out" should have been hosted by Tyndale University College, a Christian
liberal arts university with intellectual commitment to a broad range of
disciplines in the humanities and social sciences, including philosophy,
history, English literature and biblical studies—all of which are represented in this monograph.

I wish to thank the various members of the faculty who designed and
participated in this conference.

1

History, Figural History, and Providence in the Dual Witness of Prophet and Apostle

Christopher R. Seitz

AT ONE POINT IN HIS DISCUSSION OF THE WICKEDNESS CONFRONTING the prophet Habakkuk—"How long, O Lord?"—and the nations dispatched by God (Hab 1:2–11), Calvin refers interchangeably to the Babylonians and the Assyrians. It is not that he misunderstands a fundamental historical distinction with which we are familiar. It appears as though he wishes to draw upon accounts of obvious hubris and in assessing the evil rapacity of the Chaldeans in Habakkuk his mind naturally moves to the Rabshakeh's bombastic address on behalf of the Assyrian king in 2 Kings 18–19 (reproduced in Isaiah 36–37).

Assyria and Babylon are for Calvin *figures* of the selfsame divine purpose, whatever one might understand by their discrete locations in historical time. In the context of Habakkuk, where these nations replace one another in swift and agonizing fashion, Calvin is more tuned to figural history than another species of history that will emerge, in the next centuries, with a fresh acuity: a referential, punctuated history, to which the Bible is somehow externally related. It bears reflection that Calvin has no book in his library called "The History of Israel" or for that matter "The History of the World." There is no external account of "history" other than what the Bible reports, in the character of its own presentation. Calvin knows that the Babylonian empire came after the Assyrian because the Bible reports this fact quite plainly, and understanding the "historical" fact is crucial for understanding *figural history under God's providential disposing and linking.*

In time this new species of "history" would be painstakingly reconstructed, on the basis of the Bible's plain sense reference to it; by recourse to other accounts of ancient sequencing becoming available; and more importantly, as in time it was grasped that the Bible's relationship to an independent (punctuated, referential) account of "history" was no longer straightforwardly to be assumed or defended (as when challenges were leveled by the opponents of Christianity and Judaism, as from time to time had occurred). The Bible's temporal framework and "history" became different things, sometimes complementary and compatible, while at other times, as seen by those now *within* Christianity and Judaism, antagonistic and incompatible, even deceivingly so.

Defenders of a hard compatibility between these two kinds of history often unwittingly fought an "away game" with poor and ill-suited equipment, as there did not seem to be another way to think about the Bible's account of time and sequence except before a new court and jury which appeared to know something quite intimidating and threatening. (One thinks of the struggles of E. B. Pusey in his effort to salvage Daniel or the Minor Prophets against a new kind of account of their plain, now meaning *historical*, sense.) Perhaps the greatest fallout in all this was not the adoption of a defensive posture, or an inability to think about "history" along other lines. Even greater than this, it could be argued, was the loss of a vast network of internal associations within canonical scripture: literary, theological, and temporal, all at the same time. That Amos contained the same first lines with which Joel ended now no longer functioned in any natural, *configured* sense. A very complex account would have to be given that would enable the interpreter to accept a very late date for one book (Joel) and an early one for the other (Amos), even as the literary citation of the first (Joel) appears without any obvious interruption in the second (Amos). As Hans Frei showed in his penetrating account of the rise of historicism, what was true within one testament, then also became true with a vengeance as one crossed from Old to New and tried to understand the investment the second testament had in the constitutive, providentially ordered conceptuality of prophecy and fulfillment, and the material use of the Old Testament in the New.

The difficulties with constructing an external history of Israel or of the New Testament period ought not to be minimized, and that reality began to make its pressures known especially in the early history of the Old Testament. But the project was undertaken with high seriousness and the results are now before us in manifold textbooks. It is doubtful that this phase of inquiry into the Bible was avoidable, and it is questionable whether avoidance was desirable. The Bible exists in time and the events it reports, the people it shows as inspired, the audiences that first heard and the editors that received and shaped—these are historical realities in the providence of God. We fail to appreciate them only at the expense of God's own historical figuring. At issue is not this.

The sheer complexity of the historical project was especially felt when one attempted to describe in detail the genesis, development, gestation, and consolidation phases of the process of the Bible's coming-to-be, correlated now on the grid of a new historical time-line. This is not a limitation in and of itself, so long as one keeps the project focused on all phases of so-called historical development; that has however proven difficult to do. In consequence, it has been difficult to honor both the final form of the material as a piece of historical work, over against this or that previous phase of development, much less to see the final form as a distinct commentary on the character of history as all previous levels bequeath this. This also means that the text's final form and the earliest reception history of the material, as breathing one and the same historical air, is sundered, or seen only for its eccentric descriptive potential. Discontinuities are identified, and selections made concerning the true periods of value and inspiration. Though one can see little evidence of an earliest phase of reception history that insisted on the literary unity of Luke-Acts, for example, and the necessity of reading the books together, it continues to be argued that the construct Luke-Acts must be given priority as a configured and intentional work. The discussion of the limitations of this view is now forthcoming, and one can see the way in which specific nineteenth- and twentieth-century understandings of the historical task almost invariably meant a devaluing of the history of reception.

One reaction to this complexity had been a questioning of the so-called disinterested objectivity of the historical project. If readers are imposing meaning through this historical evaluation, choosing one outcome or one phase of development over another, why not set readers free to be the arbiters of meaning as such, and cut loose the so called "historical intentions" said to be there for our discovery in the first place?

Another alternative has been to find interesting all manner of literary associations in the synchronic form of the material, and to reject any developmental picture as relevant to this associative world. The Book of the Twelve is used to analyze the character of God, as one moves from book to book. Did anyone intend such a reading? Did editors or canonical forces work on the material in such a way to make this the critical lens on reading the Minor Prophets? Can we see evidence in the literary history of the Twelve that such a final form reading was what they had in mind, and if so, what is the evidence for that?

It is important to consider the contribution of figural reading with these questions in mind. It is certainly possible to engage in an analysis of the Bible that gives priority to literary associations. But a figural reading is concerned with time, every bit as much as the thinner version of historical reading is. Figural readings attend to the providential character of inspired writing and editing, in all phases of this work: both within the OT itself and then as the elected witness is filled to full by the work of Jesus Christ and then opened for the church's theological reflection across two testaments, into the present time, and as the church awaits the final consummation of promises and figures set in motion in the elected and enlarged witness of "prophet" and "apostle." It is the conviction of this author that our most recent phase of "historical reading" has been an enormous benefit, but its potential has been shortchanged. Now that we are better able to grasp the way in which the canon has developed through time, it should be even more the case that we understand the hermeneutical and theological implications of the final form of the text and the two-fold character of Christian Scripture, Old and New, Prophet and Apostle.

My own sense of the matter is that the person working the hardest to conjoin historical and theological work ("how Israel thought about YHWH") and then to harness this descriptive historical and theological evaluation with an account of God's work in time, including the witness of the NT, was Gerhard von Rad. He it was who tried valiantly to retrieve the term "typological" and link it to the sprawling historical enterprise of Introduction, History, and Biblical Theology. But it required the providential extensions of the original kerygma, revealed as phases in a tradition-historical development, to be manifestly misdrawn, as the traditions moved toward their NT fulfillment. What then, other than as vestiges of a movement whose *telos* necessitated a bending and mis-drawing of what had gone before, was the witness of the Old Testament, as the *per se* witness it was von Rad's concern to honor? Though he was not alone in recourse to typology as a means to give some sense to the two-testament world of association in Christian Scripture, now after the rise of historically thin readings, his work was the last major effort to see in typology a species of what had previously gone under the label of "spiritual sense" (allegory and figural reading both) now to be conjoined to the German interest in tradition-historical movement. And since his time, as an integrated labor of historical, literary and theological inquiry, such efforts have all but ceased.

The matter is not altogether different when one picks up the project from the other end. The OT's theological value is either determined by what the NT says about it, or by what kind of history-of-religion or tradition it hands on, finally to be adapted and transformed in the NT or the "religion of Christ followers" (whatever term is now *salonfähig*). Prophecy and fulfillment are seen as retrospectively comprehensible realities only, or prophecy is so tied to prediction that biblical studies is forced into a defensive posture in the manner of Pusey, and the figural potential of the OT as a whole is reduced to tracking a human agent predicting something and that is either being truly fulfilled on the terms of the seconding witness, or not.

Again, what is at stake in figural reading is the theological conviction that God the Holy Trinity is the eternal reality with whom we have to do, both Israel and God's adopted sons and daughters in Christ, and this has ontological as well as economic implications for our reading of the two-testament canon of Prophet and Apostle. Jesus Christ can comment on, fulfill, transform, and commend the Law only to the degree that he is its giver in the OT. The Holy Spirit, the rule of faith tells us in its earliest form, "spake by the prophets." The God who raised Jesus from the dead is not a newly revealed "Abba," in Jesus's revelatory experience, but the Father who dwells in eternity with the Son, and by the Holy Spirit interprets the cross and empty tomb and Easter all at the same time.

Reading the Old Testament according to the Rule of Faith, then, is reading it as did the earliest Fathers before the formation of the NT canon: as declaring the will of the One God, who in the latter days spoke finally and truly in the Son, the same Holy Spirit inspiring both testaments of deed, word and witness. The twofold witness of Prophet and Apostle is configured, and the church reads the scriptures in this same way so that she might understand her own place in the judgments of God, obey the commands of Christ, and lean into the promised consummation of both prophetic and apostolic witnesses.

The overreach of historical reading, then, threatened to dismantle or obscure the ontological Trinity in the name of appreciating the development and temporal movement of scripture, seen either as history-of-religion or the history of tradition. One can see the legacy of a certain species of progressivist historical conceptuality, brokered by the eighteenth- and nineteenth-century history of ideas. But does this developmental understanding connect well with the ontological claims of especially the Scriptures of Israel? In the Early Church, this witness functioned to declare the full counsel of God, in promise, law, moral injunction, figure, and indeed in a doctrine of creation said to be inherently Trinitarian in character. The second witness confirmed that this understanding of the Old Testament—call it figural—was true to its deepest character, as word both to Israel, and in Christ, a prophetic word to the church.

A proper understanding of history, on the other hand, will surely press on to appreciate the per se witness of Israel's scriptures as a word to the past, from the past, which nevertheless always contained the seeds of its own extension. The literal and figural senses were therefore historical and spiritual at one and the same time, as St. Thomas and others before him understood this. Modern figural reading wants to appreciate the highly specified character of historical time underscored by this most recent phase of the church's and academy's reflection, but then to reattach this evaluation to the two testament canon's own mature appraisal, in its given literary shape, of just what time means under the Triune God's disposing. Figural reading is then historical reading seeking to comprehend the work of God in Christ, in Israel, in the apostolic witness, and in the Holy Spirit's ongoing word to the church, conveyed now through this legacy of Prophet and Apostle, Old and New Testament, the two-testament canon of Christian Scripture.

PART ONE

Studies *in* Interpretation

2

Go Figure

Narrative Strategies for an Emerging Generation

Keith Bodner

I WOULD LIKE TO BEGIN THIS ESSAY WITH A QUOTATION, AND THOSE familiar with Ephraim Radner's recent book *Hope among the Fragments* will recognize it immediately: "The sweetest and most sublime occupation for a theologian is to search for Jesus Christ amid the sacred books [of Scripture]."[1]

As an aspiring theologian, I can certainly endorse this statement. But meanwhile, I have to earn my daily bread as a simple biblical scholar, one who plies his trade in the dust and clay of Semitic languages, putative historical context, literary criticism, and radio-carbon dating (along with an urbane avoidance of anything with the fragrance of politically-incorrect supercessionist sentiments).[2] One of the more significant pedagogical challenges during my time as a professor of Hebrew Bible/Old Testament in an undergraduate teaching context involves the quotation extracted from Radner's book, especially since my students have often asked, "So, how does one go about that task?"

For a good number of youthful students, such a task is easier done than said, and some will quickly point to a passage such as Daniel 3, and with Nebuchadnezzar, will leap to their feet in amazement: "Were there not three men that we threw into the furnace? Behold, I see four men walking around, and the fourth one looks like a son of the gods!"

---

1. Ephraim Radner, *Hope among the Fragments: The Broken Church and Its Engagement of Scripture* (Grand Rapids: Baker, 2004).

2. I am here using the term "supercessionist" as probed by Walter Brueggemann, *Theology of the Old Testament: Testimony, Dispute, Advocacy* (Minneapolis: Fortress, 1997).

Statistically, a high percentage of these same students have heard at least one sermon where it has been asserted that the fourth figure in Daniel 3 is a pre-incarnate manifestation of the Second Person of the Trinity. In my own view, this assertion does not usually proceed from a particularly well-developed Christology. But the easier route for me (in a large lecture hall) is simply to concede the example, and begin a monologue about the midterm exam.

The question of *how* to search for the Lord Jesus in the Old Testament lingers, however. And many of the same students whom I have alluded to above know, deep down, that Daniel 3 is a far easier passage to begin such a quest than many others. What about the less obvious passages? What about more difficult ones like Genesis 24, or Exodus 2, or 1 Samuel 9? How do you "look for" the Second Person of the Trinity in these texts?

In this themed-volume on "figuration in biblical interpretation," I would like to offer a few reflections suggesting that figuration is a more oft-used mode of interpretation than one might expect. As I will argue, even within the pages of Scripture itself such a mode of reading occurs. Consequently, figuration is worth commending for an emerging generation of Bible readers. In the past, such emerging readers have had other kinds of interpretation strategies bequeathed to them, often burdened with prooftexting certainties and Enlightenment sensibilities (including the requisite obsessions with provenance, authorship, and layers of composite redaction). My guess is that such reading strategies will remain with us for some time, but concomitantly, younger readers are gradually becoming interested in other ways of hearing the text. I would submit that many undergraduates are looking for wisdom to discern new rules to facilitate an enjoyment of the story, and courage to reject the questions and sentiments of a modern age, (which, quite frankly, had its own problems). I am not here interested in marketing yet another exegetical technique so much as cultivating the habit of learning to listen for opportunity to hear the gospel witness in the breadth of the canon, keeping in mind the sage counsel of *Figured Out*: "The church reads the final form of Christian scripture as canon, the parts informing the whole, the whole informing the parts, according to a rule of faith."[3]

---

3. Christopher Seitz, *Figured Out: Typology and Providence in Christian Scripture* (Louisville: Westminster John Knox, 2001) 81. There are of course other useful approaches for reading typologies of restoration between the Testaments. I am thinking of Rikki Watts, *Isaiah's New Exodus in Mark,* Biblical Studies Library (Grand Rapids: Baker, 2000) and sev-

Perhaps unexpectedly, the most helpful advocate for my thesis that figuration occurs even in the Bible itself is not featured as an author in this volume. Inconceivable as it may sound, my initial guide for this enterprise does not have the name Augustine, Gregory, Duget, Seitz, Radner, or Walters. My hero—as far as inner-biblical figuration is concerned—is none other than Joab, commander in chief of Israel's military forces in the Davidic administration. In 2 Samuel, one recalls, Joab is guilty of at least two things: homicide and figuration. Normally, one hopes these are mutually-exclusive categories, but with Joab, they seamlessly merge into one. The key episode for the present purposes occurs at the outset of chapter 11: "It was at the turn of year—the time when the messengers went forth—when David sent Joab and his servants with him, and all Israel. They destroyed the Ammonites, and laid a siege upon Rabbah, but David sat in Jerusalem." Here in 2 Samuel 11 the infamous events are well known: David sees a woman washing. "Is this not Bathsheba, daughter of Eliam, wife of Uriah the Hittite?" He lies with her, she conceives, he orders Uriah to return to Jerusalem. There is a cover-up attempt that is unsuccessful, and eventually a desperate David orders Joab to dispatch Uriah to the grave, a burial that Joab duly undertakes. It is the report of the battle in the middle of the chapter (11:18–21) that here interests me, as a summary of the siege is sent by the general to the king.

> Then Joab sent and reported to David all the affairs of the battle. He commanded the messenger, saying, "When you are finished speaking of all the affairs of the battle to the king, if it should be that the king's anger flares up, and he says to you: 'Why did you draw near to the city to fight? Didn't you know that they would shoot from the wall? Who struck down Abimelech son of Jerubbesheth? Wasn't it a woman? She threw upon him an upper millstone from the wall and he died in Thebez! Why did you draw near to the wall?'—then you should say, 'Also, your servant Uriah the Hittite is dead.'"

To my mind, it is difficult to understand this passage without an appreciation of figuration. In Joab's mode of reckoning, there is a blatant invitation to *go figure*. Abimelech (son of Gideon), according to this

---

eral essays in John J. Collins and Craig A. Evans, editors, *Christian Beginnings and the Dead Sea Scrolls,* Acadia Studies in Bible and Theology (Grand Rapids: Baker Academic, 2006).

figural interpretation, clearly stands for David.[4] In Judges 9 Abimelech is the rogue king crowned by the Shechemites, whose ignoble career is cut short when he gets nailed on the *crown* by a woman who drops an upper milestone on his head (Judg 9:53). Having been dealt this serious head injury, Abimelech then commands his armor-bearer to finish him off, lest he be subject to the eternal embarrassment of being killed by a woman. Abimelech's goal of avoiding such ridicule is evidently unsuccessful, as he becomes a bit of a byword, to the point that he can be "quoted" by a military leader as a profoundly negative example of losing one's head during the heat of battle. Here Joab, by means of figuration, is comparing the perilous actions of Abimelech with David's imprudent behavior in Jerusalem. Joab, whose career depends in large measure on David's royal stability, recognizes the folly of the king's conduct, and through this message is making a censorious statement.[5]

Furthermore, in Joab's figural interpretation the woman on the wall represents Bathsheba, while the upper millstone dropped on the king's head in Judges signifies the personal and national consequences of adultery that follows. In 2 Samuel 11, this is not a trifling affair of "consenting adults" in yet another vacuous episode of sex and the city. On the contrary, the reader can hear the larger warning in these words: Israel has a king, but the king is doing what is right in his own eyes, and there every possibility that the nation will be plummeted into the tribal chaos that marked the era of Judges, when Abimelech reigned.[6] The memory of Abimelech was earlier invoked in 1 Samuel 31, when Saul asks his armor-bearer to run him through—using the same language as Judges 9—but the armor-bearer refuses, prompting Saul to fall on his own sword. In 2 Samuel 11 David has inflicted his own self-laceration on the roof of the palace, when

4. Following Meir Sternberg, *The Poetics of Biblical Narrative: Ideological Literature and the Drama of Reading*, Indiana Literary Biblical Series (Bloomington: Indiana University Press, 1985). For an underrated study on allegory, see Joel Rosenberg *King and Kin: Political Allegory in the Hebrew Bible*, Indiana Studies in Biblical Literature (Bloomington: Indiana University Press, 1986). A thoughtful treatment on general matters of interpretation from a Jewish perspective is Michael Fishbane, *Garments of Torah: Essays in Biblical Hermeneutics*, Indiana Studies in Biblical Literature (Bloomington: Indiana University Press, 1989).

5. I have studied the role of Joab at further length in my essay, "Joab and the Risks of Reader-Response Criticism," in Bodner, *David Observed: A King in the Eyes of His Court*, Hebrew Bible Monographs 5 (Sheffield: Sheffield Phoenix, 2005) 98–109.

6. See Robert Polzin, *David and the Deuteronomist: A Literary Study of the Deuteronomic History*, Part 3: *2 Samuel*, Indiana Studies in Biblical Literature (Bloomington: Indiana University Press, 1993) 75.

he should have been at war against the Ammonites. The unhappy result of David's conduct is that the next war will not take place in the foreign lands of the Ammonites, but rather close to home within the boundaries of Israel (2 Samuel 15–19). At this pivotal time in David's career—indeed, the political and spiritual turning point of his life—figuration is used to underscore a weighty theological moment.

With Joab as an unlikely figuration inspiration, I now turn to another set of texts to sketch some further thoughts about inner-biblical figuration. I mentioned Genesis 24 a moment ago, as one of those passages where it is more challenging to search for the Lord Jesus, rather than, say, Daniel 3. Genesis 24 is the episode of Rebekah's wooing; placed immediately after the death of Sarah (and preceding the birth of Jacob and Esau), the servant of Abraham is commissioned to find a wife for Isaac among Abraham's kin.

In terms of genre, Genesis 24 is a good example of a "type-scene," an idea that has been recently popularized by Robert Alter, and can be defined as "a story pattern or situation that recurs often enough in biblical narrative so that the reader can identify a set of conventions and expectations for each one."[7] This kind of literary device occurs elsewhere in ancient literature. Literary critics point to a variety of type-scenes in Homer, such as the banquet scene, the arming of the hero for battle, and so forth. There are a number of different kinds of biblical type-scenes that scholars have identified. One useful example is the *barren wife* who gives birth to a child of destiny. We see this situation clearly in the lives of Sarah, Rebekah, Rachel, Manoah's wife in Judges 13, and Hannah, who gives birth to the prophet Samuel on the eve of Israel's request for a king. All of these stories, I would submit, have a hand in illuminating the birth of John the Baptist to aged parents in the opening chapter of St. Luke's gospel. But I will leave that analysis for another occasion, and turn instead to the betrothal type-scene of the *maiden at the well*, since Genesis 24 falls into this category. The ingredients of this particular type-scene are as follows: a potential hero is traveling away from home, and en route there is a well of water. At this

---

7. I have culled my definition from Leland Ryken and Tremper Longman III, *The Complete Literary Guide to the Bible* (Grand Rapids: Zondervan, 1993), but they are drawing on Robert Alter, *The Art of Biblical Narrative* (New York: Basic, 1981) 114–30. See also George Savran, *Encountering the Divine: Theophany in Biblical Narrative*, JSOTSup 420 (London: T. & T. Clark, 2005) 12–13. For another application, see M. S. Kee, "The Heavenly Council and Its Type-scene," *JSOT* 31 (2007) 259–73.

well are a fair maiden, some conflict, and a moment of resolution followed
by a consummation of the flirtatious dynamic with the maiden. We now
pick up the story of Abraham's servant and his journey in v. 10:

> [10] Then the servant took ten of his master's camels and departed
> with all kinds of gifts from his master at his disposal. He journeyed
> to the region of Aram Naharaim and the city of Nahor. [11] He made
> the camels kneel down by the well outside the city. It was evening,
> the time when the women would go out to draw water.

> [12] He prayed, "O Lord, God of my master Abraham, guide me
> today. Be faithful to my master Abraham. [13] Here I am, standing
> by the spring, and the daughters of the people who live in the town
> are coming out to draw water.

> [14] I will say to a young woman, 'Please lower your jar so I may
> drink.' May the one you have chosen for your servant Isaac reply,
> 'Drink, and I'll give your camels water too.' In this way I will know
> that you have been faithful to my master."

> [15] Before he had finished praying, there came Rebekah with her
> water jug on her shoulder. She was the daughter of Bethuel son
> of Milcah (Milcah was the wife of Abraham's brother Nahor).
> (NET)

In this paragraph one can observe the requisite elements for the betrothal type-scene. To begin with, it is the servant of Abraham who sets
out on a journey to the distant land of his master's ancestry in search of a
bride, rather than the prospective groom himself, Isaac, who is represented
by proxy in this episode. It could be argued that this representation by the
servant fits in well with Isaac's overall characterization. As Robert Alter
has mentioned on several occasions, Isaac is manifestly the most passive
of the patriarchs. Furthermore, the *object* of this journey is matrimony.
Most often, (as we will have occasion to see), matrimony is ancillary to
the character's reason for making the journey in the first place, and merely
"happens" as events unfold. But in Genesis 24—the first of the betrothal
type-scenes—the goal of marriage is foregrounded at the outset. A slight
complication occurs when the servant, having reached the spatial destina-
tion of the city of Nahor, encounters a score of maidens. In the context
of a prayer, the servant devises a divinely-ordained test to enable the right
choice to be made. The prayer is answered even before it ends, so to speak,

as Rebekah arrives on the scene, and meets all the criteria: she fills her water jar, and as the servants gives thanks to God, she runs to tell her family the good news. The type-scene gradually moves toward its resolution, as Rebekah (after a protracted negotiation) is secured as a wife for Isaac, and makes the return journey to Canaan.

In terms of the Genesis plotline as a whole, it is entirely appropriate that a type-scene occurs at this particular place in the narrative. Starting in chapter 12, God speaks to Abram and makes a wild promise that is global in scope, eternal in length, and reiterated on numerous occasions: through this man's descendents, every other family on earth will blessed. In Genesis 24, Abraham's descendent—his son Isaac, through whom this promise will be realized—finds a wife, and thus the promise moves one small step closer toward its fulfillment. Even amidst the seemingly mundane routine of drawing water, it is possible for a design plan to be discerned. Such a notion is confirmed a few chapters later, when another betrothal type-scene transpires in Genesis 29. While the same basic ingredients are seen in Genesis 29 (potential hero traveling, well of water) there is also some innovation that can be noticed. George Savran's discussion is thus helpful, since he understands a type-scene as "a recurrent scene within a story whose repetitions reveal both identity and difference: identity in the basic plot sequence that is described, and difference in the deployment of certain motifs in varying fashion."[8] Consequently, the reader should be on the lookout for such variation in the betrothal type-scene as Genesis 29 intersects with the antecedent text of chapter 24 on a figural plane. Again, the placement of the type-scene in Genesis 29 is strategic within the overall narrative: Jacob just had the dream of Bethel, where God has disclosed that he is the "heir" of Abraham's promise. Continuing his journey, the inheritor of the promise is about to encounter his future bride, enabling the promise to continue toward fulfillment.

> [1] So Jacob moved on and came to the land of the eastern people. [2] He saw in the field a well with three flocks of sheep lying beside it, because the flocks were watered from that well. Now a large stone covered the mouth of the well. [3] When all the flocks were gathered there, the shepherds would roll the stone off the mouth of the well and water the sheep. Then they would put the stone back in its place over the well's mouth. (NET)

8. George Savran, "Theophany as Type Scene," *Prooftexts* 23 (2003) 125.

The reason Jacob is fleeing is because of the stolen blessing and the wrath of his brother Esau. Rebekah herself forges the plan for Jacob to take refuge with Laban, and the pretext for his trip abroad—so the mother says—is that she is disgusted with life because of Esau's Hittite wives. Although matrimony is purported reason for the trip, one senses that this is more of an excuse than a reason, and ironically, Jacob himself will eventually return home with two wives. But many things will have to happen before Jacob actually gets married, and as chapter 29 begins, it is still a somewhat precipitous moment in his life. As soon as chapter 29 opens, the ingredients of a betrothal type-scene are apparent, as the potential hero (Jacob) is traveling away from home, and stumbles upon a well of water. The strained dialogue with the local shepherds might represent a level of conflict in the story (or perhaps the large stone over the mouth of well), but in v. 9 the maiden then enters the stage:

> 9 While he was still speaking with them, Rachel arrived with her father's sheep, for she was tending them. 10 When Jacob saw Rachel, the daughter of his uncle Laban, and the sheep of his uncle Laban, he went over and rolled the stone off the mouth of the well and watered the sheep of his uncle Laban. 11 Then Jacob kissed Rachel and began to weep loudly. 12 When Jacob explained to Rachel that he was a relative of her father and the son of Rebekah, she ran and told her father.

> 13 When Laban heard this news about Jacob, his sister's son, he rushed out to meet him. He embraced him and kissed him and brought him to his house. Jacob told Laban how he was related to him. 14 Then Laban said to him, "You are indeed my own flesh and blood." So Jacob stayed with him for a month. (NET)

The betrothal type-scene in Genesis 29 functions as both a reminder of the providential design (just as in the Isaac/Rebekah example above) and as part of the great guarantee that God keeps his promises even against the odds or despite lapses on the part of his people. To be sure, it is not accidental that *marriage* is involved, and one strongly suspects that this is symbolic of God's covenant with his people. The spatial setting of the well also plays a role. While some might argue that the well is simply the ancient Near Eastern equivalent of a coffee shop or gathering place (albeit with the practical utility of drawing water), one also might understand the well as a classic image of fertility: a place that facilitates putting the "spring" back into "offspring," so to speak. While there are common elements to the betrothal scene, the differences can be the most interesting literary part. Even from these two examples, we can see that episodes such as these are not rigidly imposed, but rather there is a dynamic flexibility at work, with creative variation based on individual and circumstance, as well as the theological rhythms of the story. Such variation should be kept in mind when considering the next text. I have recently argued that 1 Samuel 9:11–13 exploits the conventional betrothal type-scene imagery.[9] By way of background, the elders of Israel have asked for a king in the previous chapter, and now the son of Kish from the marginalized tribe of Benjamin is about to be anointed king. In this episode in the first part of 1 Samuel 9, Saul and his servant lad are in search of lost donkeys, and are searching for the seer to aid them in their quest:

> Now just as they were going up the hill toward the city, they found some girls coming out to draw water, and they said to them, "Is the seer here?" They answered them, and said, "Yes, he's right in front of you! Hurry! Now! Indeed, today he has arrived at the city, for today there's a sacrifice for the people at the high place. Just as you enter the city, you'll find him before he goes up to the high place to eat, for the people won't eat until he comes for *he* will bless the sacrifice after thus the invited ones will eat. So now, go up, indeed, him today you'll find him!" And they went up to the city. Now just as they were entering the midst of the city, behold, Samuel was coming out to meet them, to go up to the high place.

Here in 1 Samuel 9, Saul—the potential hero, as Israel's first king—is on a journey away from his home, and encounters a group of maidens coming out to draw water. Like the servant of Abraham in Genesis 24, there is a spiritual dimension to the language, as they ask for directions to the seer. The long response of the females sounds like a discordant symphony, and the Hebrew text is fraught with awkward syntax, as though the girls are all speaking at the same time. Such excitement that is conveyed through

---

9. Bodner, *1 Samuel*, Readings (Sheffield, forthcoming). In this section of the commentary, I am drawing on suggestions by Alter, *Art of Biblical Narrative*, and Shimon Bar-Efrat, *Narrative Art in the Bible*, JSOTSup 70 (Sheffield: Almond, 1989). My painfully literal translation is indebted to the study of Gary Rendsburg, "Confused Language as a Deliberate Literary Device in Biblical Hebrew Narrative," *Journal of Hebrew Scriptures* 2 (1999) Article 6 <http://www.purl.org/jhs>)—who maintains that the Hebrew syntax reflects multiple speakers talking all at once.

the text is perfectly appropriate for a betrothal type-scene of Israel's first king. However, it can be observed that the type-scene in 1 Samuel 9:11–13 does not come to its expected resolution. Instead of some further interaction with one of the maidens, the next sentence in the story reads: "And they went up to the city. Now just as they were entering the midst of the city, behold, Samuel was coming out to meet them, to go up to the high place" (9:14). At the conclusion of the dialogue, Saul does not move into a relationship with one of the excited young girls; instead, he gets a meeting with the prophet Samuel, a grumpy old man. Consequently, a number of scholars have labeled this episode in 1 Samuel 9 as "an aborted type-scene." A critical reader could demur that in chapter 13 Saul already has a grown son Jonathan (and in 14:50 it is revealed that his wife's name is Ahinoam), so it is curious that a type-scene should occur here when it is not strictly necessary, as with Isaac and Jacob. So why is it here?

After reading the book of 1 Samuel in its entirety, one concludes that the aborted type-scene becomes symbolic of Saul's reign—Saul's kingship is aborted in a not dissimilar manner as this encounter with the maidens. In fact, you could say that this episode functions as a kind of Saul's royal vocation, where things really do not go very well. In terms of national leadership and destiny, Saul will not have a career like Isaac, Jacob, or Moses. Robert Alter provides a poignant summary, "the deflection of the anticipated type-scene somehow isolates Saul, sounds a faintly ominous note that begins to prepare us for the story of the king who loses his kingship, who will not be a conduit for the future rulers of Israel, and who ends skewered on his own sword."[10] This episode comments on Saul's overall characterization, and foreshadows the end of his reign before it even begins. Furthermore, I have argued that the aborted type-scene becomes an emblematic image of the disastrous marriage between Israel and kingship. The aborted type-scene thus draws attention to some of the wider implications of Israel's experiment with kingship and the "husband" language that one finds in many places in 1 Samuel. To appropriate the argument of Jon Levenson, kingship can certainly represent an alternative embrace for Israel, an embrace that will ultimately result in exile from the land of promise.[11] Therefore, in addition to the argument that this aborted type-scene is symbolic of Saul's personal problems (not all which

10. Alter, *Art of Biblical Narrative*, 60–61.

11. Jon D. Levenson, *Sinai and Zion: An Entry into the Jewish Bible* (Minneapolis: Winston, 1985) 70–80.

are his fault, it must be said), it also signals the disastrous impact of Israel's forsaking her covenant partner in favor of dalliance with kingship. Such an argument is enhanced, to my mind, when the events of Exodus 2:15–21 are considered:

> [15] When Pharaoh heard about this event, he sought to kill Moses. So Moses fled from Pharaoh and settled in the land of Midian, and he settled by a certain well. [16] Now a priest of Midian had seven daughters, and they came and began to draw water and fill the troughs in order to water their father's flock. [17] When some shepherds came and drove them away, Moses came up and defended them and then watered their flock.
>
> [18] So when they came home to their father Reuel, he asked, "Why have you come home so early today?" [19] They said, "An Egyptian man rescued us from the shepherds, and he actually drew water for us and watered the flock!" [20] He said to his daughters, "So where is he? Why in the world did you leave the man? Call him, so that he may eat a meal with us." [21] Moses agreed to stay with the man, and he gave his daughter Zipporah to Moses in marriage. (NET)

Exodus 2 has a number of intertextual points of contact with preceding narratives in Genesis. For instance, Moses' mother places him in an "ark," and the only other occurrences of this word in the entire Bible are in Genesis 6–9, the story of Noah's ark. Just as Noah is a passenger in a boat loaded with cargo having salvific import, so now the very young Moses is floating on the waters of chaos in a fragile vessel that carries the promise of God. Still, upon landing on the shores of the Nile, Moses can be considered an unlikely hero: reared in Pharoah's house, and guilty of voluntary manslaughter as he flees to the land of Midian. It is a fortuitous moment in the story, therefore, when Moses experiences a betrothal type-scene; armed with a prior reading of similar episodes in the lives of Isaac and Jacob, the reader can immediately see the currency of this kind of type-scene for Moses at this particular moment in sacred history. Fleeing from Pharoah, Moses may seem like a no-hoper until he rather innocuously sits down by a well. Not only that, but this priest of Midian has seven daughters making it virtually impossible for this type-scene to fail (even if Moses is, as he will claim in the next chapter, a poor speaker who has "foreskinned lips"). At what would seem to be the lowest moment in Moses' life, the type-scene works as memorable reminder that God will honor his covenant with Abraham, with Isaac, and with Jacob, and has no intention of giving up on the people of Israel despite their present misfortunes. For Moses himself—despite exile in Midian and life as a fugitive—he has a role to play in the saving of many lives because he has had an encounter at a well just like his ancestors. This continues the theme of God's promise finding its fulfillment in unlikely places, and thus the type-scene of Exodus 2 makes an important theological contribution to the unfolding narrative. On balance, a key point about a type-scene is that it shows the creativity of God in keeping his promise to Abraham: "Through your descendants every family on earth will be blessed." Type-scenes have a habit of occurring when God's promise looks especially threatened or less likely to be fulfilled.

The question of this essay surrounds the issue of searching for the Lord Jesus even in the scrolls of the Hebrew Scriptures. In terms of pedagogy, or even homiletics, how does one go about this task? After all, as Radner warns:

> . . . if we cannot search for—and somehow come to find—Jesus in Genesis and Acts *together*, in Leviticus and Philemon, in 1 Samuel and Jude, in Job, the Psalms, Nahum, and in Revelation, *and with the same particularity* as in the Gospels, then we have not yet opened ourselves to the forming of our spirits by the Holy Spirit of God, the author of life and word together.[12]

Christopher Seitz explores the same question: "as von Campenhausen has stated (in a paraphrase from Childs), 'the problem of the early church was not what to do with the Old Testament in the light of the gospel, which was Luther's concern, but rather the reverse. In the light of the Jewish scriptures which are acknowledged to be the true oracles of God, how were Christians to understand the good news of Jesus Christ?'"[13] To respond to this challenge, I am submitting that inner-biblical figuration provides an angle of insight, and for a final example I turn to St. John's gospel. Of course, one does not have to read further than the first three words ("In the beginning") to discover how early moments in the gospel narrative are configured in terms of the Hebrew Scriptures.[14] Even before

---

12. Radner, *Hope Among the Fragments*, in a similar vein as the quotation that begins this essay.

13. Seitz, *Figured Out*, 188.

14. Several relevant issues are discussed in Dan Lioy, *The Search for Ultimate Reality:*

the opening chapter has drawn to a close, the reader is given a vision of "Jacob's ladder," as Nathaniel is told that he will see greater things than this. Inner-biblical figuration is a major part of the literary and theological design; in other words, it is through the lens of inner-biblical figuration that the gospel writer would have us see the Lord Jesus in earlier passages such as Genesis 24. In light of the above discussion about the betrothal type-scene, consider these selected verses from John 4:

> [3] . . . the Lord . . . left Judea and went back once more to Galilee.
>
> [4] Now he had to go through Samaria. [5] So he came to a town in Samaria called Sychar, near the plot of ground Jacob had given to his son Joseph. [6] Jacob's well was there, and Jesus, tired as he was from the journey, sat down by the well. It was about the sixth hour.
>
> [7] When a Samaritan woman came to draw water, Jesus said to her, "Will you give me a drink?" [8] (His disciples had gone into the town to buy food.)
>
> [9] The Samaritan woman said to him, "You are a Jew and I am a Samaritan woman. How can you ask me for a drink?" (For Jews do not associate with Samaritans.)
>
> [10] Jesus answered her, "If you knew the gift of God and who it is that asks you for a drink, you would have asked him and he would have given you living water."
>
> [11] "Sir," the woman said, "you have nothing to draw with and the well is deep. Where can you get this living water? [12] Are you greater than our father Jacob, who gave us the well and drank from it himself, as did also his sons and his flocks and herds?"
>
> [13] Jesus answered, "Everyone who drinks this water will be thirsty again, [14] but whoever drinks the water I give him will never thirst. Indeed, the water I give him will become in him a spring of water welling up to eternal life."

Intertextuality between the Genesis and Johannine Prologues, Studies in Biblical Literature 93 (New York: Lang, 2005). For a helpful study in the book of Matthew, see Michael P. Knowles, "Scripture, History, Messiah: Scriptural Fulfillment and the Fullness of Time in Matthew's Gospel," in *Hearing the Old Testament in the New Testament,* edited by Stanley Porter, McMaster New Testament Studies (Grand Rapids: Eerdmans, 2006) 59–82.

[15] The woman said to him, "Sir, give me this water so that I won't get thirsty and have to keep coming here to draw water."

[16] He told her, "Go, call your husband and come back."

[17]"I have no husband," she replied. Jesus said to her, "You are right when you say you have no husband. [18] The fact is, you have had five husbands, and the man you now have is not your husband. What you have just said is quite true."

[*Fast forward to verse 52*]

[25] The woman said, "I know that Messiah" (called Christ) "is coming. When he comes, he will explain everything to us."

[26] Then Jesus declared, "I who speak to you am he." (NIV)

At the risk of belaboring the obvious, the elements of the betrothal type-scene are clearly evident here in John 4. Jesus is traveling, and Samaria is a region outside the land of promise.[15] In this episode, the well of water is teeming with symbolism, since it is referred to as "Jacob's well." There are several layers of conflict in this transaction: issues of ethnicity, theology, and even gender-relations surface in the dialogue. So the requisite elements are in place, but at the same time, it must be said that the woman of Samaria does not need a conventional betrothal type-scene; she has had apparently had plenty of those already. Far more than a conventional husband, the Fourth Evangelist is saying, this woman needs the living water that springs forth when one is part of the bride of Christ. The profusion of dialogue in John 4 seems to go beyond the usual conventions of the type-scene. Rebekah is fairly active in Genesis 24, but the Samaritan woman is highlighted to a far higher degree, (yet for all that, her name is not disclosed). The reader can immediately spot both continuity and variation with betrothal type-scenes we have looked at, as Gail O'Day summarizes: "In John 4, the Messiah comes not only to Israel, but also to those whom Israel marginalizes and despises. Unlike the OT type-scenes of the maiden at the well, Jesus does not come to the well looking for a woman to be his [wife], but for a witness who will recognize the Messiah and invite the

---

15. For a recent study on the historical background, and extensive bibliography, see Gary K. Knoppers, "What has Mt. Zion to do with Mt. Gerizim? A Study in the Early Relations between the Jews and the Samaritans in the Persian Period," *Studies in Religion/Sciences Religieuses* 34/3–4 (2005) 307–36.

despised people to himself."[16] In the economy of the gospel, there can be some remarkable surprises.

John 4 is more than just a remarkable literary achievement and more than just a literary appropriation; the type-scene is part of the theological configuration of the text, teaching the church how to engage the Scriptures, and, paraphrasing a great theologian, instructing us in how to uncover God in all corners of its textual universe. The type-scene unites diverse parts of Scripture, and the Fourth Evangelist deploys a fund of resources from earlier texts to arrive at a transforming conclusion. The unnamed woman, in the end, goes on to be a witness in her village: "Then the woman left her water jar, went off into the town and said to the people, 'Come, see a man who told me everything I ever did. Surely he can't be the Messiah, can he?'" (4:28–29, NET). Stan Walters once asked me: why, in v. 28, does the Samaritan woman leave her water jar? With all the assets of canonical criticism, I will hazard a guess that *she had to*. The betrothal type-scene of the maiden at the well is now over: it has now reached its consummation, and across all these scenes, the various parts testify to the whole. In John 4, the unnamed Samaritan woman has found the Messiah—the covenant partner—and hence, as readers, we will not need that water jar again *in the canon of Scripture*. Abandoning the jar at the well powerfully suggests that the source of living water has been found, and fulfillment of the ancient promise has arrived. Therefore, the literary technique ultimately becomes a handmaiden to the highest discernment. I am now prepared to agree with Ephraim Radner, who intones: "The Scriptures themselves, written by a sublime author, reflect his order and coherence and unity amid diverse parts and periods. And they do so in the ways that reveal the echoes and shadows and figures of Christ, resonating within Old and New Testaments, thematically organizing, imagistically interconnecting, narrationally weaving a unified vision of God's being within the world that is perfectly given in the incarnation." Radner then concludes, "And thus, to enter this orchestrated and divine reality is to be changed by an encounter with a grace that converts the intellectual and

16. Gail R. O'Day, "The Gospel of John," in *New Interpreter's Bible*, vol. 9 (Nashville: Abingdon, 1996) 565. A literature review can be found in Jocelyn McWhirter, *The Bridegroom Messiah and the People of God: Marriage in the Fourth Gospel*, SNTMS 138 (Cambridge: Cambridge University Press, 2006). More generally, see Tom Thatcher, "Remembering Jesus: John's Negative Christology," in *The Messiah in the Old and New Testaments*, edited by Stanley Porter, McMaster New Testament Studies; Grand Rapids: Eerdmans, 2007) 165–89.

spiritual being of the reader." When we read in such a manner, surely there are new possibilities for the broken church and its emerging generation to *go figure* that there is hope *within* the fragments.[17]

17. Radner, *Hope among the Fragments*, 97.

3

The Truth that Casts Out Fear

A Sermon on Leviticus 12 and Luke 2:21ff

Ephraim Radner

IF ANY TEXT IN LEVITICUS HAS AN IMMEDIATE AND OSTENSIVE CONNEC-tion with the Gospel, it is this text of Chapter 12. Even the discussion on the Day of the Atonement in chapter 16, though it may appear more central, theologically, in its association with the sacrifice of the Cross in Paul's language, or in Hebrews' exposition of the Great High Priest—even this represents a relationship that is broad in its significance, and imprecise in its mirroring of the Levitical text. But *here*, certainly, in chapter 12's details of childbirth and purification and circumcision, we have the actual particularities of Mary and Jesus' actions described in their religious speci-ficity, as laid bare in Luke 2:21–23: they are enacting *this* word of Moses, and none other. Enacting it and, in this "fulfillment" of it, establishing its truth in all the world (cf. Matt 5:17; Rom 10:4).

Even the Roman Catholic Church has set aside a feastday bound to this Levitical specificity: the Purification of the Blessed Virgin Mary, appointed for February 2, and measured precisely from the Nativity as the text allows us to do. Yet something odd took place with this day, something that marks our own readings of this text I suspect. St. Anthony of Padua, the first follower of St. Francis who became a teaching theologian in the thirteenth century, said this in a sermon for the Purification: "The Lord spoke to Moses, in Leviticus 12, saying: If a woman having received seed shall bear a man child, she shall be unclean seven days [Lev 12:1–2]. This is in distinction to her who gave birth as a virgin. Neither the child nor the mother needed to be purified by sacrifices; it was to free us from the fear of the Law, that is, from keeping a law which is observed in fear."[1] Odd indeed: Moses commands, yet Mary is free from the command's purpose, and only follows in order to show us *not* to follow. What were we afraid of, in any case, in this text?

Anthony was only following the tradition here, dating back to Origen. For the great exegete of Leviticus had himself noted that the text in 12:2 applies to a "woman who conceives/receives seed and bears a male child," but since Mary, as a "virgin" was touched rather by the Holy Spirit and did not receive any semen she is therefore not impure. "Let regular women bear the burden of the Law, but let virgins be exempt," he writes. And having distinguished Mary in this way—and by implication the child that she bears—Origen then lays aside the evangelical meaning of the text, and seeks to explain Leviticus "on its own terms," as he puts it. Why the impurity of childbirth for all other women? Because of the inherence of sin in conception and birth itself, he insists. Later Christian interpreters as we know, following Augustine, made much of this, attaching the transmission of sin to the sexual act itself which, as everyone pointed out, first took place only outside of Eden.

Thus, the text, both in Leviticus and Luke, proved something of a problem in the face of Mary's asserted virginity and Christ's own sinlessness. And the Catholic tradition as a whole, thereafter, used the texts less as illuminating revelations than as an occasion to *distinguish* between Leviticus 12's referents and the actual birth of Jesus, thus differentiating Jesus from other men, but also, more and more, separating Mary out from other women. Assertions that, for instance, Mary's womb miraculously closed again following Jesus' birth, and that no blood or placenta emerged from her body, soon became standard claims, thereby placing the matter of childbirth described in Leviticus within an "ancient" realm of covenantal (and still-fallen human) anachronism.

One might think that Protestants would recoil at such readings, and they did, worrying that this differentiation had gone too far in subsuming Mary into its net. Sensibly observing that Mary herself in fact performs the purificatory ritual demanded of a new mother, they countered their Roman Catholic adversaries by insisting that Mary too was "stained" by original sin—no "immaculate conception" here. She is just like all the rest of us. Jesus, however and of course, was not. Interpreting circumci-

---

1. *Homilies of St. Francis*, trans. Paul Spilsbury (Mansfield, MA: Franciscan Archives, 1979).

sion (Lev 12:3) as an "atoning" rite for the male, Christian interpreters tended to explain its application in Jesus' case as a kind of "fulfillment of righteousness" on his part, much like his baptism (cf. Matt 3:15), a demonstration to others of his willingness to obey, even if, for his own person, unnecessary in itself. Hence, especially in Protestant hands, the Levitical rites described in Luke 2 are seen as pedagogical signs for a more general moral attitude—what I call "moral allegory"—but in themselves as "ineffective" ones. After all, there is no original sin to atone for in our births any more. There is blood, to be sure; but the blood is now uninteresting.

It should come as no surprise if, in modern times among Catholics and those Protestants like the Lutherans and Anglicans who follow the traditional calendar, the Feast of the Purification of the Virgin has changed its name: we now call it the Presentation, and so peel off the entire scene from its literal meaning. Catholic and Protestant exegesis together have used the texts as launching pads to doctrinal concerns that have their own logic and origins, with the result that it is unclear why we read these texts at all. The all-too-neat division of law and abrogation has, not surprisingly, left much of the Old Testament—and in this case, some of the New Testament too—to the realm of historical curiosity. And yet . . . Mary *purifies* herself, and offers sacrifice, for the birth of *her* Son, whose name is Jesus. Not in general; but for him. This she does, just as Leviticus says she must. No comment is offered, and no hint that there is something here to be explained, as in Jesus' baptism. No, it is done, just as all the deeds of patriarch, prophet, and Messiah are done—in the open, before the sight of God and angels.

I mentioned in my talk earlier (see p. 103) that the figural reading of the Bible is in part bound up with our own need to be changed, be challenged in our hearts, to be judged, condemned, and remade. For Pascal, as I indicated, this calling is aimed straight at the demands of our corruptions and our weaknesses. If we will not read this text as "true" at its root, it can only mean that we are running from a truth we need to hear, that is, that we have fear lurking behind its meaning that threatens to be exposed. "Not Mary!" we exclaim; "not you, Lord!" like Peter in the face of the first revelation of his Master's path and passion. "Get behind me, Satan!" the Lord responds.

For Tertullian, the fear this text instills in us is clear and strikes deep into the heart of our relationship with God. To the Gnostic Marcion, he lifts up the mirror of this, just in the terms of Luke 2 and Leviticus 12:

Come now (Tertullian writes to Marcion in his combative treatise *On the Flesh of Christ*), beginning from the nativity itself, declaim against the uncleanness of the generative elements within the womb, the filthy concretion of fluid and blood, of the growth of the flesh for nine months long out of that very mire. Describe the womb as it enlarges from day to day, heavy, troublesome, restless even in sleep, changeful in its feelings of dislike and desire. Inveigh now likewise against the shame itself of a woman in travail which, however, ought rather to be honored in consideration of that peril, or to be held sacred in respect of (the mystery of) nature. Of course you are horrified also at the infant, which is shed into life with the embarrassments which accompany it from the womb; you likewise, of course, loathe it even after it is washed, when it is dressed out in its swaddling-clothes, graced with repeated anointing, smiled on with nurse's fawns. This reverend course of nature, you, O Marcion, (are pleased to) spit upon; and yet, in what way were *you* born? You detest a human being at his birth; *then after what fashion do you love anybody?*" (4)

How do you love anyone?, Tertullian asks. This woman, covered in blood and fluid, the baby, smeared, wet, slippery with the mass of his mother's insides—it is a kind of *love* we fear in this text, is it not? A kind of love that we would run from. What love in fact? The love of sinner, the love of creature, the love of the lost and of the repellant and of the infinitely distanced from God.

I hardly exaggerate here. For this scene and its physical *stuff*, if you will, that Origen would not touch and Anthony would not let us linger over, goes to the heart of the Incarnation itself, and it is Leviticus 12 that tells us this. Jewish commentators have perhaps sensed this better than we. How is it, the Rabbis ask when speaking of this text, that the most nauseating sight, frightful in its pain and shocking in its literal mess, should, in the form of an infant just out of the womb and suffused in the slime of its creaturely element, how is it that, without a moment's hesitation, all around move to this child, pick it up, hold it, wipe it, wrap it, and hug it with cries of joy and affection (*Leviticus Rabbah*)? The answer they give? It is one of the greatest miracles of God's salvation visible in the world of men and women: this is a mark of *God's* love, nothing less. Love for the world, love for creature, love for you and me, love for Israel.

Is this not what the prophet tells us? "This is what the Sovereign LORD says to Jerusalem: Your ancestry and birth were in the land of the Canaanites; your father was an Amorite and your mother a Hittite. On the day you were born your cord was not cut, nor were you washed with water to make you clean, nor were you rubbed with salt or wrapped in cloths. No one looked on you with pity or had compassion enough to do any of these things for you. Rather, you were thrown out into the open field, for on the day you were born you were despised. Then I passed by and saw you kicking about in your blood, and as you lay there in your blood I said to you, 'Live!' I made you grow like a plant of the field. You grew up and developed and became the most beautiful of jewels. Your breasts were formed and your hair grew, you who were naked and bare" (Ezek 16:3–7).

Leviticus 12 may or may not tell us anything about the Immaculate Conception. But it *does* tell us about the Incarnation—fundamentally, it speaks to us of the relationship of creature and even creation to God, established and laid out to view in the birth and incarnation of Jesus Christ. Everything is contained here: from Eve's travail, "multiplied in sorrow and conception" (Gen 3:16), to the travail of Israel and her hapless prophets— "for I have heard a voice as of a woman in travail . . . the voice of the daughter of Zion that bewails herself" (Jer 4:31)—to the travail of the Messiah himself—"a woman when she in travail has sorrow, because her hour is come, but as soon as she is delivered of the child, she remembers no more her anguish, for the joy that a man is born into the world, and now ye therefore have sorrow, but I will see you again, and your heart shall rejoice, and your joy no man taketh from you" (John 16:21–22)—to the travail of the church itself as bound to and as the Body of Christ—"And there appeared a great wonder in heaven: a woman clothed with the sun, and the moon under her feet, and upon her head a crown of twelve stars; and she being with child cried, travailing in birth, and pained to be delivered' (Rev 12:1–2), or, as Paul writes, "I rejoice in my sufferings for you, and fill up that which is behind of the travails of Christ in my flesh for his body's sake, which is the church" (Col 1:24). Who should we love? Is not the one who is loved by God? Where shall we love? Is it not from Eve even to this place? How shall we love? Is it not as God loved us—this is love, not that we loved God, but that he loved us and sent his son . . . just here, just in this way? (1 John 4:10).

We have been reflecting on "figuralism" these past days. Let us be clear: figuralism is not an exercise in correlating objects and referents in the Bible. It is rather an openness to all of history as being filled with the body of Christ. And thereby, and in no other way, does the truth cast out our fear.

4

Finding Christ in the Psalms

Stanley D. Walters

As an interpreter of scripture, I've felt for some time—maybe about twenty years!—as if I'm on a long portage. After traveling many miles on the waters of historical interpretation, I've dragged my canoe up the bank and onto my shoulders and headed for the next lake. I'm sure the two bodies of water are connected, but there's no easy passage between them, and so I'm going overland. In fact, the whole guild of biblical studies stands between epochs; some people are already there, up ahead, pulled in at the dock of Camp Figuration, and some are still back there, happily moored at Rancho Wie-Es-Eigentlich-Gewesen (I think that's an Ojibway expression), or, to translate it, Rancho As-It-Really-Was.

To find Christ in the Psalms was the aim—or at least the result—of the earliest Christian writers, namely, Paul and the gospels, and, according to them, this practice goes back to Jesus himself and to those who knew him best in his earthly ministry.

From that beginning until the modern hegemony of the historical-critical tradition, in various ways and sometimes with sophisticated theories of meaning, Christians found Christ in the psalms, especially in the so-called royal psalms and in the other material associated with David. But strict historical interpretation limited the meaning of those texts to what David and others like him could have known. Since Jesus lived many centuries later, the psalms could hardly be speaking of him.[1]

---

1. "The majority of modern scholars are fully in accord with Gunkel and Mowinckel in rejecting the traditional interpretation of messianic psalms" (Brevard S. Childs, *Introduction to the Old Testament as Scripture* [Philadelphia: Fortress, 1979], 515).

This essay is about doing what the historical-critical tradition never really allowed, namely, accepting second meanings for written texts found in the book of Psalms. In part 1 I offer the general grounds that second meanings arise through a semantic shift when a text comes to stand in a different context. In parts 2 and 3 of the paper, more briefly, I introduce two specific grounds, namely, that the book of Psalms seems to have been edited with a messianic interest, and that Jesus himself seems to have found his own work in the Old Testament.

By a text, I mean *a group of written or spoken words that belong together because of a common theme and design.* The biblical psalms are such texts, a prophetic oracle such as Isa 10:5–19 is such a text, a narrative such as 1 Sam 30 is such a text.

By "context" I mean *the specific circumstances of human culture—both human and literary—in which a text has its currency and in which its meaning must be discerned.* And I do assume that one determines the sense of a text through an interactive social process between a) the text, b) the interpreters (readers or hearers), and c) the social or literary context within which interpreters seek the text's meaning.

Second Meanings through Semantic Shifts

Changed Contexts

I begin with two examples of changed contexts that do not involve the Bible.

A Yale University student was visiting China at the time of the event at Tianamen Square, June, 1989. In a moving first-hand report made upon his return, he told of hearing a Chinese student in Beijing passionately declaiming Martin Luther King's "I Have a Dream" speech. The speaker was in public, surrounded by other students, and when his memory faltered, his friends prompted him. They all seemed to know the speech, and clearly appropriated its words and power to their own personal and political situation.

The "text" here is King's speech given August 28, 1963, and its original context was the situation of blacks in the U.S. south at that time. No doubt Chinese students saw similarities between those circumstances and their own—twenty-five years later and on the other side of the globe. Historical analogy prompted them to appropriate it, but its referent is now clearly different. In its new location, in both time and place, King's text refers to a situation about which he knew nothing whatever. It retains its historical meaning, of course, but its new location gives it fresh force and requires an additional level of meaning it had never before borne.

Here is a second example. On January 10, 1984, the Wendy's hamburger chain aired a new TV advertisement comparing its own product with that of a rival chain. Three elderly ladies examine a hamburger, a tiny patty on a huge, puffy bun. Two of the ladies poke it, exchanging bemused comments: "It certainly is a *big* bun," one says, and the other says, "It's a big *fluffy* bun." The third, an actress named Clara Peller, interrupts them with her outraged demand, "Yes, but where's the beef?"[2]

The ad became hugely popular, and played a role in the U.S. presidential primaries that same spring. Among the Democrats, senator Gary Hart had moved ahead of Vice President Walter Mondale in the polls, making repeated reference to his "new ideas." In a televised debate, Hart once again used his slogan, and Mondale leaned forward to say, "When I hear your new ideas I'm reminded of that ad, 'Where's the beef?'"

To speak historically, those three words are a text from early 1984 referring to hamburgers. But in its early change of venue, a semantic shift occurs in which this text's force is entirely different: it now refers to political goals and policies. In the plain sense of Clara Peller's question, "beef" means beef; but in the context of political rhetoric—same country, same time, same words—it displays a derived sense. It is no longer just about food, but also about the Democratic platform. This is instant figuration, and it happened when someone planted down in a different circumstance that statement, "Where's the beef?" forcing it to become a type and not just a word.[3]

These examples show that words are susceptible to multiple meanings depending on the circumstances in which they exist. To state the same thing differently, a change of circumstance may lead a given text to yield a different meaning.

The historical sense of any text depends on the context in which it was composed. But when a text is reused—the instances given above involve persuasion and wit—a different context may require the text to display a different sense. "Require" is not too strong a term, since it is

2. Based on information in http://en.wikipedia.org/wiki/Where%27s?the?beef%3F.

3. I've made earlier use of this instance, see Stanley D. Walters, "The Needy is King: Preaching with a Contextual Hermeneutic," *Toronto Journal of Theology* 5(1989): 88–89.

precisely the second meaning that gives the text its new power. It would be utterly jejune for Chinese authorities to reply that the Chinese can sit anywhere on the bus they choose, or for Hart to ask Mondale where he went for lunch.

When we, people of the twenty-first century, study biblical texts historically, we make the effort of imagination necessary to substitute for our own cultural context the ancient context in which the text originated. And, clearly, more than imagination is needed, for one must also know enough about that other context to be realistic about the text's meaning in that setting. Thus, the historical reader must be both well-informed about that other time and place, and also capable of sympathetic disengagement from his/her own context and engagement with the historical context. The historical meaning of the text is guided, even constrained, by what those words and patterns signified in that setting.

Biblical scholarship working in this vein has achieved extraordinary knowledge of the languages in which the Bible is written, and of its multiple times-and-places. Readers of no other ancient texts are as favored as the Bible's readers in this respect, and I suppose that the Bible's readers are more favored today than they have been at any other time in history. When we read the Bible in this way, we are seeking its *original* sense, its *historical* sense, its *plain* sense.

The Bible is often read in no other way; much of the academic reading and study of it proceeds only in this way. I think that such an historical reading of the Bible is essential—but not sufficient.

When we turn from these contemporary examples to the Bible, we find similar changes of context. Every attempt to preach from the Bible involves one, but the changes of context that bear on interpreting the Bible go so far back in time that they begin in the life of God's people even before the writing of the Bible was complete. In fact, the writing of the Bible is one of two major changes of context that affect our interpretation; the other has to do with kingship. The effects of the two seem to be intertwined, and I turn first to kingship.

Kingship

According to the biblical narrative, Israel adopted a political kingship in the days of Samuel and Saul, sometime around 1000 BC, and it endured for something over four centuries. The literary deposit of Israel's kingship includes the Bible's narratives of kings in the books of Samuel, Kings, and Chronicles, and a group of texts often called "royal psalms." There must also have been foundational documents of some sort, and protocols and procedures, but none of these have survived. Samuel developed a Kingship Code, doubtless embodying the prophet's theocratic reservations about kingship in Israel, and made it public by depositing it at the sanctuary (1 Sam 10:25). But this seems to have disappeared with Saul's kingship, which it was created to guide and support.[4]

From the royal psalms, to be sure, scholars at mid-twentieth century postulated liturgies for various royal ceremonies, such as the anointing and enthronement of the king, and they interpreted the royal psalms as part of those ceremonies.[5] But those ceremonial events are, for us, largely hypothetical, and we actually know the royal psalms only from their presence in the book of Psalms, where their function is quite different.

Samuel had finally been convinced, in spite of the bad Canaanite examples, that there could be a king who would be pleasing to God (1 Sam 10:25). Saul proved not to be that king, but for a time it looked as if David might be. But even Israelite kingship was a statue with feet of clay, and at least from the moment that was clear, Israelite kingship became susceptible to a derived sense pointing to the King to come.

Kings and kingship in Israel came to an end with the destruction of Jerusalem in 586 BC. This is a radical change of cultural context. For us, the question is, What could be the meaning of royal texts when royalty is no more? Shall they be preserved, in hopes of political restoration? Shall they be saved for antiquarian reasons? Or, what else?

Once kingship was gone, royal texts could retain *their original sense* only for those hoping for a return of the same political kingship that Israel once possessed. But there were always those in Israel who believed that kingship was an act of disloyalty to God, and whose hopes for a future kingship took a messianic rather than a dynastic direction. In addition, as any kind of restoration post-586 tarried—Jehoiachin never resumed the throne, nor did

4. In my view, Samuel's rebuke, "You have not kept the commandment of the Lord your God, with which he commanded you" (1 Samuel 13:13), refers to Saul's violation of a provision or provisions of this Code.

5. See, e.g., Sigmund Mowinckel, *The Psalms in Israel's Worship. Volume 1*, D. R. Ap-Thomas, translator (Oxford: Basil Blackwell, 1962), 61–76.

anyone else in David's line—the future hopes of Israel's royalists would have increasingly turned to messianic rather than dynastic hope.[6]

The disappearance of kingship, then, is the new cultural context that effects a semantic shift in Israel's royal texts: they refer to the King who is to come—and that reference constrains what those texts can mean.

Psalm 45

This leads me to a third example of semantic shift in changed context, this time from the Bible—Psalm 45.

The psalm's superscription calls it a "love song," and it reads that way. After complimenting the king on his good looks and military prowess, the text speaks of his "ivory palaces," of his scepter and scented robes, and of musical instruments that make him "glad." It also addresses the queen, calling her a princess and speaking of her "robes interwoven with gold" and of her "virgin companions." "The king will desire your beauty," it says, urging her, "[F]orget your people and your father's house," "[E]nter the palace of the king" "with joy and gladness." In closing, the poem assures the king, "In place of your fathers shall be your sons; you will make them princes in all the earth."

Historical-critical study calls it a wedding song for the king. "The poem," says Oesterley, who doubts it should even be called a psalm, "offers an illuminating picture of a royal wedding in ancient Palestine,"[7] and, thinking of a commentary's function, he adds, "The subject-matter of this psalm does not call for a section on religious teaching."[8] And who should disagree? This is the plain sense of that psalm.

6. There seems to me no reason that the development of messianic hope necessarily depended on a political kingship in Israel. It could well have been part of the long discussion on Israel's governance that the Exodus and Israel's emergence as a people must have triggered. The insistence on God's kingship antedated the political institution in Israel, and there may well have been those in the decades following Moses' death who could envision a heaven-sent teacher and ruler in the mode of Moses but who would refuse a human king. When, historically, this took place one can hardly determine, but the strong messianic spin apparent in the book of Samuel points to the early tenth century. I should think it originated within the mind and heart of Samuel himself, something the transmitting tradition never forgot, so that even the book of those narratives must (oddly) bear his name. Indeed, the disposition to hope largely for the future characteristic of Israel's best thinkers could in itself have triggered messianic hope.

7. W. O. E. Oesterley, *The Psalms. Translated with Text-Critical and Exegetical Notes*, reprint, 1939 (London: SPCK, 1953), 250.

8. Oesterley, 254.

But traditional Bible-readers know that the king and his bride have usually been understood as figures for Christ and the church, and an old gospel song adopts the psalm's language in speaking of Christ as one who came "out of the ivory palaces into a world of woe." Nor were Christians the first to make such a move, for already Jewish interpreters had regarded the king as the Messiah,[9] and the queen as Israel.[10]

This would be a second meaning of the royal wedding song. Following the defeat by Nebuchadnezzar, Israel's thinkers had three options: give up the royal texts altogether, preserve them for antiquarian reasons, or accept the constraint of a changed context and allow their figural reference to the King who is to come.

We should notice how the text's present location confirms this shift, an observation that returns us to the Psalms as a literary document. Psalm 45's neighbor on the left, Psalm 44, speaks of a tragic defeat that has befallen Israel, lamenting it as divine rejection in spite of the people's faithfulness. The language is strong and dark.

> . . . you have rejected us and disgraced us
> and have not gone out with our armies. . . .
> You have sold your people for a trifle,
> demanding no high price for them. . . .
> All this has come upon us,
> though we have not forgotten you,
> and we have not been false to your covenant. (Ps 44:9, 12, 17)

On the right, however, Psalm 46 speaks of God's deliverance of Jerusalem in language of extravagant confidence:

> There is a river whose streams
> make glad the city of God,
> the holy habitation of the Most High.
> God is in the midst of her, she shall not be moved;
> God will help her when morning dawns.
> The nations rage, the kingdoms totter;

9. The Targum of Psalm 45:3 reads, "Your beauty, O King Messiah, is more excellent than that of the sons of men." Delitzsch says that "mighty God" in Is 9:5 refers back to Psalm 45. Franz Delitzsch, *Biblical Commentary on the Psalms. Second Edition.* Vol 2, David Eaton, translator (London: Hodder and Stoughton, 1902), 85.

10. "The verses beginning *Hearken, O daughter, and consider* (45:11), to the end of the Psalm are spoken to the congregation of Israel" William G. Braude, translator, *The Midrash on Psalms. Vol 1* (New Haven: Yale University Press, 1959), 454.

he utters his voice, the earth melts. (Ps 46:4–6)

Why should the wedding song be slipped in between those textual opposites? What is it that can move Israel from a calamitous rout in Ps 44 to glorious global victory in Ps 46? Well, even as a wedding song this poem would tell you that Israel's king has something to do with the victory. In a military crisis, he's the one on the spot—newly-wed or not! Go ahead with the wedding, but forget the honeymoon! But then, Ps 46 speaks of a victory without military engagement; it says that God "makes wars to cease to the end of the earth," and it quotes the divine declaration, "I will be exalted among the nations // I will be exalted in the earth!" The scope and finality of these words suggests a victory no mere David can win. This is the Messiah's work.

I think the rabbinic-Christian readings of Psalm 45—they are *re-readings*, really—originate in Israel's changed circumstances following 586 BC, and so the psalm can stand in where a reference to the Messiah is wanted. But even if it were still only a royal wedding song, the new literary context—between *O God, we have heard* and *God is our refuge* (to resort to incipits in place of numerals)—would force the semantic shift through which the earthly king becomes a figure for the King who is to come.

Semantic Shift

In all three of these examples I'm speaking of the capacity of written or spoken text to *contain* or to *acquire* additional meaning beyond the historical sense of its words, under the constraint of a changed context—a changed cultural context, and a changed literary context. This is a feature of language as we know and use it, especially in wit and humor and in passionate, persuading speech. It's what I've spoken of as a semantic shift. The plain sense moves over to make room for another.

Here is a homely metaphor. When I was in graduate school I walked to the university library every day, about a thirty-minute walk each way. I have long legs and can move at a good pace, but one morning I heard rapid steps coming up behind me—not running, pelting steps, but small steps, very close together, and faster than I thought it possible to move your legs. I didn't think it polite to turn around and look, so, maintaining my own pace, I just moved over to let the walker by. Shortly there breezed past me a small woman dressed in a sari, beating out that tattoo with her feet that was going to get her to work on time even if I would be late.

I moved over.

This is a metaphor in space for what can happen to words and meanings in our heads. Beef means hamburger means beef—until it feels the approach of a political debate over ideas and policies, and it has to shift to one side a little and make room. Beef now refers to cogent principles and plans for national life.

Similarly, Psalm 45 is a wedding song until Psalms 44 and 46 move up on it; they crowd around, push and shove a little—and an interesting text on Palestinian wedding customs becomes a picture of the Messiah, linked to the believing community. Psalm 45 does not change; rather, I find myself obliged to understand it differently. There is another level of meaning.

The presence of levels of meaning in our use of language supports the reasonableness of finding Christ in the psalms. I do not argue that the writer of Psalm 45 or the redactor of Book II of the Psalter, through divine inspiration, knew about Jesus. In this I am still paddling on historical waters. Nor am I at this time arguing that God, through providential guidance of the biblical writers, led them to use words especially suitable to future meanings of which they were as ignorant as was Martin Luther King of Tianamen Square—although that is a serious position. I argue now only that changes in the placement of biblical texts—in history and culture, and within other written texts—make them susceptible to additional levels of meaning that may include reference to Christ.

With Tianamen Square, the text has moved, through space (to China) and with passage of time (twenty-five years). With Walter Mondale, the text has changed cultural and social contexts without moving much in time. With scripture, say Psalm 45, the text moves, mentally, into the king-deprived life of post-exilic Israel, and physically, throughout the whole process of gathering and editing that has given us the two testaments of the Christian Bible. Historical-critical methods help us theorize about that process of gathering and editing, and practitioners of those various criticisms have shown great linguistic and historical learning, along with great skill in imaginative inference. It has also often seemed that their work stopped just short of what it means for those who look to it to hear God's voice.

These two changes of context—two ways that can hardly be separated from one another—make it plausible to find second meanings in the ancient words of the biblical psalms. "Scripture" is the premier example of the re-use of texts.

Messianic Editing of the Psalms

In addition to that general hermeneutic ground, there are two specific grounds for finding Christ in the Psalms: First, already within ancient Israel the canonical book of Psalms appears to have been edited and shaped to express (among other ideas) Israel's messianic hope, and second, Jesus himself seems to have found his own work in the psalms.

Edited and shaped. The canonical Psalter shows features that imply a self-conscious vision of the book as a whole and its continuing role. It reached this form through a process of collection and arrangement that extended throughout Israel's continuing use of the psalms in worship, devotion, and study. (Think of the way the works of any poet can be published and republished in successive collections differing from one another and usually increasing in size. If the author is still living, earlier collections could not have contained the still-unwritten poems, and later collections can omit poems deemed unsuitable for any reason, and can even provide a different principle of arrangement.) The subdivision of the Psalms into five numbered segments, often themselves called "books," is one such feature of arrangement.

Messianic hope. The specific feature of the Psalter's arrangement that is pertinent here has to do especially with the "royal" psalms, They number a dozen or so,[11] and I assume that they originated at the time of Israel's monarchy and functioned during that period with reference to the kings of Israel and Judah.[12] This would be their plain or historical sense. Psalm 2, for example, has been described as part of the "anointment ritual" for the installation of the Israelite king.[13]

The royal psalms, however, instead of standing more or less as a group,[14] are scattered throughout the Psalter.

Psalms 72 and 89 stand at break-points between the five books, effectively bracketing Book III, the middle of the five books. Within it, for

---

11. Limburg lists 2, 18, 20, 21, 45, 72, 89, 101, 110, 132, 144:1–11 James Limburg, "Psalms, Book Of," in *The Anchor Bible Dictionary. Vol V* (New York: Doubleday, 1992), 533. Mowinckel had included also 28, 61, 63, "and quite a number of others," and did not include 144 (Sigmund Mowinckel, *The Psalms in Israel's Worship. Volume 47 (1.*

12. So Limburg.

13 Mowinckel, 63.

14. As do the *ma'alot*-psalms, for example, or the hallelujah-psalms at the close of the book, or the kingship-psalms in the 90's, or the Davidic laments (concentrated in Book I and Book II, as well as in the resumptive group 138-145).

the first time, the Psalter admits references to the destruction of Jerusalem and the burning of the Temple in 586.[15] Psalm 72, associated by its superscription with Solomon, speaks glowingly of the ideal king and of the blessings of his rule to the people. Psalm 89 speaks extravagantly of God's covenant with David as king, although with a twist to which I return in a moment.

Psalm 89 is important for us at this point, and I pause a moment over it. The last psalm in Book III, its first 37 verses celebrate God's dynastic promise to David:

> I have sworn to David my servant [God says]:
> I will establish your offspring forever,
> and build your throne for all generations, (vv. 3–4)

and then,

> Once for all I have sworn by my holiness;
> I will not lie to David. (v. 35)

The first part of the psalm is so positive on David's kingship that a lectionary can assign it to Advent 4, Christmas Sunday.

But then, in v. 38, the psalmist begins to address God in bitter complaint and to assert quite the opposite:

> But now, you have cast off and rejected; . . .
> You have renounced the covenant with your servant;
> you have defiled his crown in the dust. . . .
>
> Where is your steadfast love of old,
> which by your faithfulness you swore to David? (vv. 38, 39, 49).

The psalm's ending is as dark and tragic as its earlier part is bright. The impression left by it, Gerald Wilson observes, is "of a covenant remembered, but a covenant *failed*. The Davidic covenant introduced in Ps 2 has come to nothing." And Books I–III of the Psalter conclude "with the anguished cry of the Davidic descendants."[16]

---

15. Psalm 74:4-8 reads as if dependent on eye-witness testimony. Psalms 44 and 60 are indeed rejection psalms found earlier in the psalter, but neither seems to reflect the catastrophe of 586.

16. Gerald H. Wilson, *The Editing of the Hebrew Psalter*, SBL Dissertation Series (Chicao, CA: Scholars Press, 1985), 213.

Book III is framed by 72 and 89, which pair of psalms we may characterize, respectively, as the vision and the reality, as kingship at its best and at its worst, and as kingship working and kingship failing.

In short, the dark realism of Psalm 89 testifies that kingship in Israel is finished. This historical fact had a profound hermeneutic effect upon Israel's scriptures.

The process of the Psalter's editing continued long past the existence of Israel's historical kingship. The Babylonians destroyed Jerusalem at the beginning of the sixth century BC, and Israel returned from that Exile at mid-century; the events of post-exilic life narrated in Ezra and Nehemiah belong to the fifth century. Indeed, evidence from the Qumran literature—the Dead Sea Scrolls—suggests that the editorial activity on the book of Psalms was probably still under way in the period of the New Testament.

What interest do Jewish believers of the first century—centuries after kingship had disappeared forever from Israel—have in ancient poems about their kings? I answer resolutely, These people are forming Scripture, not gathering artifacts for a museum. In preserving psalms of kingship, they are providing for the instruction and spiritual nurture of God's people. This points to the royal psalms as bearers of messianic hope. What I argued for Psalm 45 was happening to all the royal psalms: their continuing use in study, devotion, and worship implies that they have taken on a second meaning that refers them to the King who is to come.

And so the drastic change of historical context in 586 is matched by the changed literary context as the book of Psalms grows and takes its present shape. In response to seismic changes in Israel's life, the royal psalms have all "moved over," as earthly kingship becomes a figure for the rule of God through the King who is to come. Childs speaks of "the attachment of new meaning to the older vocabulary through the influence of the prophetic message (cf. Jer 23:5; Ezek 34:23)."[17] These shifts follow upon the destruction of Jerusalem in 586 BC and the consequent disappearance of kingship as an Israelite institution. Although the royal psalms spoke originally of the historical kings, "They were treasured in the Psalter for a different reason, namely as a witness to the messianic hope which looked for the consummation of God's kingship through his Anointed One."[18]

17. Childs, *Introduction to the Old Testament as Scripture*, 516.
18. Childs, 517.

Many interpreters have followed Childs in this. Rendtorff, for example, "There can be no doubt that at this stage they [the royal psalms] were understood in messianic terms: the praise of God is not only directed to the past and the present, but also includes the messianic future."[19] "When there were no longer reigning kings in Israel, the psalms written for use in royal ceremonies were re-read as divine promises and prophecies of a future messiah (see the comment on Psalms 2; 89; 110)."[20]

This is the book Jesus and the Twelve read and knew. It was not Peter and John who made the Psalms a messianic book; that had happened before. As the disciples came to believe that Jesus was the Messiah, it was inevitable that they should read the psalms as speaking of him. The transition was seamless.

The Bible now exists—in Christian belief—in a world where the Messiah has come. Christians who believe that Jesus is the Christ will interpret these texts, the royal psalms, of Him. Wherever Christians find messianic hopes in the Old Testament, they know who the person is who fulfills them. It would not be wrong to call this a further derived sense, another level of meaning. But, given the facts of history, for many Christians, the derived sense is the literal sense.

Many interpreters have said that Psalm 2 joins Psalm 1 as an introduction to the Psalms, and specifically guides us to read the Psalter as having to do with the hope of God's people for the Age to Come under God's anointed Son. The Psalter, then, is a book of praise, Teaching, and messianic hope.

Christ and the Psalms

In my third point I argue that we may find Christ in the psalms because he did so himself. In this assertion we find ourselves on more familiar and traditional ground.[21]

We know those places in the New Testament. "You search the Scriptures" Jesus says to some of his critics in the aftermath of the healing at the Pool of Bethesda, "because you think that in them you have eternal

19. Rolf Rendtorff, *The Old Testament: an Introduction* (Philadelphia: Fortress, 1986), 249.

20. James L. Mays, *Psalms*, Interpretation (Louisville: Westminster John Knox, 1994), 11.

21. See especially the thorough and lasting study, Richard T. France, *Jesus and the Old Testament. His Application of Old Testament Passages to Himself and His Mission* (London: Tyndale Press, 1971).

life; and it is they that bear witness about me . . ." (John 5:39), and a few sentences later, "If you believed Moses, you would believe me; for he wrote of me" (v. 46).

And again, on the Emmaus road, Luke tells us, "Beginning with Moses and all the Prophets, [Jesus] interpreted to them in all the Scriptures the things concerning himself" (24:27). Cleopas and his companion say that Jesus "opened to us the Scriptures" (v. 32). And in the closing lines of the gospel, Jesus reminds a group of his followers that he had always told them "that everything written about me in the Law of Moses and the Prophets and the Psalms must be fulfilled" (v. 44).

Jesus makes it sound as if he's everywhere in the Bible.

Yet the critical tradition never found it easy to say that. For one thing, higher criticism was never convinced that it knew exactly what Jesus had said. And the Jesus Seminar, that high-water mark of historical-critical study, has made many people more doubtful than ever.

And for another, early practitioners of the historical-critical tradition found that Jesus' views of the Old Testament documents were pre-critical and far too simple. His views were those of his time, and even if one were sure of what he said, modern knowledge (it was thought) surpasses ancient knowledge and understands the true historical meaning of those Old Testament texts.

In the twentieth century, the best way through the latter conclusion, assuming it was troublesome, was to assert that, in his incarnate state, Jesus of course suffered the same limitations of knowledge as everyone else. Campers at Rancho As-It-Really-Was were told, "Jesus didn't come to teach us higher criticism." The incarnation and its costly sacrifices had to do with redemption; methods of interpretation we could figure out for ourselves.

a. As to the former question—Do we really know what Jesus said?— apologists of great learning have long addressed it. I speak briefly for myself in the following paragraph before returning to the second question.

To be sure, the earlier Gospels stand perhaps three decades from Jesus' own time. Yet his followers transmitted his words and works through that period in a public process that offers safeguards against gross alteration of the apostolic testimony. Witnesses, both friendly and hostile, to Jesus' ministry, would often have been present as Christians proclaimed the Good News, and integrity led Jesus' followers to distinguish between their own views and his (1 Cor 7:10, 12). And there were undoubtedly written memoranda and proto-gospels prior to the works we know as the canonical Gospels. The earliest church trusted the latter implicitly. These grounds give me general confidence as I read them.

b. To return to the limitations of Jesus's knowledge, one notes with embarrassment the twentieth-century western assumption that we moderns know better than the ancients in almost everything. But even given normal human limits to Jesus's knowledge, openness to levels of meaning helps us greatly on the historical level. A text such as that cited in Matt 2:15, "Out of Egypt I called my son" (Hos 11:1), easily accommodates an enlargement of reference such as the Martin Luther King speech undergoes in my opening example.

But it goes deeper than this, and includes questions such as, What is necessary to understand the Bible as scripture? Is it possible so to understand it without knowing the panoply of critical observations that still gives the guild of biblical scholarship its distinctive character? And to what understanding of the Bible do those observations alone admit one?

A recent writer has noticed what he calls "the ever-growing irrelevance of biblical studies in academia." Writing as an exercise in "ideological criticism," Hector Avalos thinks it improper "that biblical studies [in the academy] is still functioning as a handmaiden to theology and faith communities rather than as a discipline relevant to those outside of faith communities." As he sees it, biblical studies as an academic discipline actually has no importance outside the church, and is "doomed to irrelevance in secular academia"; "reappropriation" of the biblical text by academic scholars "is essentially a charade that should end."[22]

These assertions show no conception of the formative role of the Bible in western civilization, including the system of university education in which we have all been formed, or of humanistic learning as beneficial to the individuals that accept it. But it is correct that it is "communities of faith," i.e., Jews and Christians, who have a stake in the Bible. This raises old and very long questions about interpreting the Bible, and especially about the authority of the secular academy. One remembers that Tertullian denied that those who do not stand within the apostolic tradition even possess the Scriptures.[23] The people for whom the Bible truly

22. Avalos, "The Ideology of the Society of Biblical Literature and the Demise of an Academic Profession," *SBL Forum* May 24, 2006 1-4.

23. See Ronald Heine, in Frances Young, Lewis Ayres, editors, *The Cambridge History of Early Christian Literature* (Cambridge: University Press, 2004), 135; David Dockery,

matters are those linked to it within the confessional and sacramental life of the people of God. That's our circle; it has Jesus Christ at its center, and we know ourselves redeemed through him in a plan of the triune God revealed to us in holy Scripture.

And here I return to Jesus's view of the Old Testament. He seems to have understood his own mission in terms provided by that Bible, especially Isaiah's figure of the suffering servant. The Old Testament formed and guided the work Jesus did and the death that he died. *In trusting ourselves to that mission we have already trusted ourselves to his reading of scripture.* It seems to me, therefore, that in seeking Christ in the psalms we are also walking where he walked and seeking to read as he read. We declare ourselves part of the apostolic tradition in whose care Jesus's Bible became known as the Old Testament and reaches us as Christian Scripture.

I admit there are still a lot of questions. Is Jesus everywhere in the Old Testament? or just in those royal psalms? And is he everywhere in those psalms, or only there where the New Testament finds him? Justin Martyr found a lot of lines in Psalm 22 that the gospel writers didn't use! And, What will stop people from wild allegorical flights that embarrass us rather than nourish our minds and hearts? These are questions for another paper, although the Rule of Faith is close at hand, and the history of interpretation shows us that it's possible to hold together the primary and the derived senses of a text in a responsible way—without which, we lose the use of the psalms for our own personal comfort and direction.

To return to the portage: Water seeks its own level; and, although I may be paddling in a different lake, I'm still concerned to learn what historical methods can teach me. And I'm not really looking for a port, somewhere safe to tie up and hide out. But I now notice that the horizons are wider. This is a spacious lake, and it seems to me that somehow the portage has put me back in the main stream, reading the Bible to hear God speak, and to know and love his Son.

Biblical Interpretation then and Now. Contemporary Hermeneutics in the Light of the Early Church (Grand Rapids: Baker, 1992), 70.

Bibliography

Avalos, Hector. "The Ideology of the Society of Biblical Literature and the Demise of an Academic Profession." *SBL Forum*, May 24, 2006.

Braude, William G., translator. *The Midrash on Psalms*. Vol 1. New Haven: Yale University Press, 1959.

Childs, Brevard S. *Introduction to the Old Testament as Scripture*. Philadelphia: Fortress, 1979. (For the Psalms, see "The Psalms," 504–25.)

Delitzsch, Franz. *Biblical Commentary on the Psalms*. 2nd ed. Vol 2. David Eaton. London: Hodder and Stoughton, 1902.

Dockery, David. *Biblical Interpretation Then and Now: Contemporary Hermeneutics in the Light of the Early Church*. Grand Rapids: Baker, 1992.

Limburg, James. "Psalms, Book Of." In *The Anchor Bible Dictionary*, edited by David Noel Freedman, 5:522–36. New York: Doubleday, 1992.

Mays, James L. *Psalms*. Interpretation. Louisville: John Knox, 1994.

Mowinckel, Sigmund. *The Psalms in Israel's Worship*. Translated by D. R. Ap-Thomas. Oxford: Blackwell, 1962. Reprinted, Grand Rapids: Eerdmans, 2004.

Oesterley, W. O. E. *The Psalms. Translated with Text-Critical and Exegetical Notes*. 1939. London: SPCK, 1953.

Rendtorff, Rolf. *The Old Testament: An Introduction*. Translated by John Bowden. Philadelphia: Fortress, 1986.

Vanderkam, James, and Peter Flint. *The Meaning of the Dead Sea Scrolls*. San Francisco: Harper, 2002.

Walters, Stanley D. "The Needy is King: Preaching with a Contextual Hermeneutic." *Toronto Journal of Theology* 5 (1989) 88–103.

Wilson, Gerald H. *The Editing of the Hebrew Psalter*. SBL Dissertation Series 76. Chico, CA: Scholars, 1985.

Young, Frances, Lewis Ayres, editors. *The Cambridge History of Early Christian Literature*. Cambridge: University Press, 2004.

5

"Gone Astray"

Dealing with the Sotah *(Num 5:11–31)*

Nathan MacDonald

IT IS A COMMON PERCEPTION THAT WHAT IT MEANS TO READ ACCORD-
ing to the literal sense is self-evident and that this way of reading stands
over against figural or allegorical readings. In reality, nothing could be
further from the truth. This perception owes a great deal to what Rowan
Williams has described as the "disastrous shrinkage" of the literal sense
to the historical sense in the modern period that Hans Frei mapped so effectively in his *Eclipse of Biblical Narrative*.[1] The literal meaning of the text
was singular and equated with its historical or ideational referent, without
remainder. As it happens this was an unhappy state of affairs for religiously
interested critics who felt that the biblical text held relevance for their contemporaries. In such a context they were often reduced to uncontrolled
analogies "of the most spiritualizing and moralizing sort" in order to give
the historically reconstructed biblical text ongoing significance.[2] In other
words, what resulted was not a loss of figural readings, but the adoption of
a particular and reified form of figuration. Such examples are salutary and
evidence that what is at stake is not the distilling of a truly literal reading
uncontaminated by any hint of allegory, but the appropriate coordination
of literal and figural.

The following paper examines one particular biblical text and the
forms in which this coordination of literal and figural has taken place
during the history of interpretation. The biblical text is the *Sotah*, the test
for the wife suspected of unfaithfulness, which is found in Num 5:11–31.

---

1. Williams, "Discipline," 48; Frei, *Eclipse*.
2. Seitz, *Figured Out*, viii.

The benefit of a dialogue with the history of interpretation is that it places modern interpretations in a new light, exposing the extent to which these readings fail to be "literal," despite assumptions to the contrary. Many modern interpretations of the *Sotah* exemplify the "disastrous shrinkage" of the literal sense. Those that recognize the hermeneutical deficiency of such myopia and seek the text's contemporary significance actually under-mine the literal sense, though it is often assumed that the interpretations being offered are according to the literal sense. Consequently, I will con-clude with an attempt to repristinate a figural interpretation that takes its direction from a literal reading of the *Sotah* in its canonical context.

The Wife Suspected of Unfaithfulness

In Num 5–6 we find a series of legal texts placed within the larger narrative context of Israel's sojourn in the wilderness of Sinai (1:1—10:10). One of these texts is the *Sotah* (5:11–31), which takes its name from the Hebrew verb "to go astray." "This is the law for jealousy when a woman goes astray (*tiśṭeh*) from her husband and makes herself unclean, or when a spirit of jealousy comes over a man and he suspects his wife" (5:29–30).[3] As this concluding colophon makes clear, the wife is suspected of adultery by her husband, and the text describes the ritual the woman may be required to undergo if such suspicions arise.[4] The description of the ritual evidences considerable effort to describe in detail what steps are to be taken by the priest administering the ordeal. This quest for precision results in a com-plex and repetitious text, which is best examined in five sections.[5]

The introduction outlines the conditions for the ordeal (vv. 11–14). The husband suspects that his wife has been unfaithful to him. He has no witnesses that this is the case, which prohibits access to the usual judicial proceedings since these required the testimony of at least two witnesses (Deut 17:6). The preparations for the ritual ordeal are described in vv. 15–18. The woman's hair is dishevelled by the priest—indicating her pos-sible shame and uncleanness; into her hands is placed a grain offering—composed without oil or incense, like the sin offering (Lev 5:11);[6] and,

---

3. Translations mine, unless otherwise noted.

4. Thus no definitive judgement is passed about the guilt of the wife. This is despite the NIV's, at best, ambiguous title for the section: "test for an unfaithful wife."

5. Milgrom, *Numbers*, 351–54.

6. "Because the sacrifice now offered is to be accomplished on no joyful occasion";

the priest presents to her the bitter water made with sanctuary dust. At the heart of the passage is the ritual oath (vv. 19–24). The priest utters the curse in the form of an oath, which the woman takes upon herself with the words "Amen, amen." The priest then adds the words of the curse to the bitter water. In vv. 25–28 the ordeal itself takes place. The woman drinks the bitter water and the grain offering is burnt on the altar. The effect of the bitter water is described. If she is guilty there will be some terrible effect on her reproductive organs, if she is innocent she can continue to bear children. Finally, the passage concludes with a colophon, which redescribes the conditions for the ordeal adding that, whatever the result, the husband will not suffer any consequences.

The "Disastrous Shrinkage" of the Literal Sense

The "disastrous shrinkage" of the literal sense to the historical sense is well illustrated by the *Sotah* in the hands of some modern commentators. For our purposes Martin Noth's classic mid-twentieth century commentary on the book of Numbers can serve as a parade example. For Noth, the *Sotah* is a primitive ritual that has been lightly reworked by the priestly writer. His comments are almost entirely on the level of historical description.[7] Much of what Noth has to say about the passage concerns the technical problems that the passage presents to the interpreter.

There are three types of problems with which modern interpreters have been forced to wrestle. First, Noth observes the relative uniqueness of this ritual. "Nowhere . . . is there found an exact parallel to the present legislation. The whole gives a markedly primitive impression and certainly goes back to a fairly ancient practice."[8] Within the biblical text the ordeal in Num 5 is without parallel. It is possible, however, to compare it to ordeal rituals in the rest of the ancient Near East. Thus, for example, in Babylon and Mari there existed a cold-water ordeal in which the suspect was thrown into a river. Secondly, the presence of a primitive ritual in the post-exilic work of the priestly writer suggests the existence of compositional layers. This is confirmed by the repetition and inconsistencies that characterize the text. "The contents of the section obviously had a pre-literary history. For in the present version of the procedure two or

---

Philo, *Spec. Laws* 3:10.

7. For other examples, see Davies, *Numbers*, 48–57; Gray, *Numbers*, 43–56.

8. Noth, *Numbers*, 49.

even three different kinds of divine judgement are so closely amalgamated that they can no longer from the literary point of view, be separated."[9] Thirdly, some of the vocabulary in the text is opaque and requires philological investigation. The recurring expression *mê hammārim hame'ārarîm* (vv. 18, 19, 22, 24, 27) is translated by Noth as "the curse-bringing bitter waters"[10] The word *mārîm* is difficult, Noth observes, but is probably to be rendered "bitter." In this he agrees with most scholars and follows the Vulgate by relating *mārîm* to the root *marar* "to be bitter," rather than the Septuagint which reads "water of disputation." The Septuagint's rendering understands *mārîm* to be from the root *marah* "to be rebellious, contentious," and was revived in modern times by G. R. Driver.[11] The sacrificial term, *azkarah* (vv. 25, 26), is "no longer comprehensible."[12] Interestingly, Noth passes over the difficulty of ascertaining the nature of the curse the woman endures. Other modern commentators have been more intrigued by "your thigh will drop and your belly swell" (vv. 21, 27), understanding it as an imprecise reference to a medical condition, perhaps a prolapsed uterus, or a euphemism for an abortive pregnancy. Whether the curse concerns sterility or an abortion cannot be considered aside from the positive reflex: "she shall be able to bear children" (v. 28), which may be taken to imply either continued fertility or an unterminated pregnancy. If the woman is understood to be pregnant, this might suggest that what led to the husband's suspicions was a pregnancy which he did not believe had resulted from their marital relationship.

In his analysis of these historical and philological issues Noth is, of course, as surefooted as we would expect from one of the great Old Testament scholars from the middle part of the twentieth century. In contrast, Noth's interpretative contribution is unsatisfactory as he rarely ventures beyond an attempt to describe as precisely as possible the nature of the ritual envisaged by the priestly writer. The possibility that this ritual might or better, should exercise his, one must assume, largely Christian

9. Ibid. Stade first drew attention to these difficulties, see Stade, "Pentateuchkritik." More recently, a number of scholars have discerned instead a unified composition. See, especially, Brichto, "Case"; Fishbane, "Accusations"; Milgrom, "Case."

10. "Das fluchtbringende Bitter-Wasser" (Noth, *Numeri*, 47).

11. Driver, "Two Problems." Sasson's suggestion "waters that bless and waters that curse" has justifiably not found favour ("Numbers 5"). Similarly, Brichto's derivation from *yarah* "waters of revelation" ("Case," 59 n. 1).

12. Noth, *Numbers*, 51.

readership, for whom this text is part of sacred Scripture, appears to be of little concern to Noth. There is, however one exception where he notes the ritual's location before YHWH and observes, "with the mention of the name of Yahweh, the procedure, wherever its origin is to be sought, is drawn into the realm of the Old Testament conception of faith."[13] It must surely be the case that this must have far-reaching implications for the assessment of Israel's God and Old Testament, but Noth refuses to be drawn further into the possible implications of this observation.

It would, of course, be common among many biblical scholars to ask what else Noth should be expected to do. Rex Mason describes this attitude perfectly.

> Strictly speaking, it is the Old Testament scholar's brief to try to explain as well as he or she can just what he thinks the biblical author is saying. When that is done he or she can bow off the stage in thankful anonymity, concealed in a smokescreen of objectivity. If we go on to ask, "Does what the biblical writer is saying here make any sense?", or "Is there any way it can possibly be relevant or even 'true' for later times?", the scholar is no more equipped than anyone else to answer.[14]

The fact that Noth's lack of interpretative comment would in no way be considered remarkable among Old Testament scholars illustrates the domestication to the "disastrous shrinkage" of the literal sense that characterizes many modern readings. Yet, Noth's reticence cannot be left to stand, a matter pressed upon us most strongly in recent years by feminist writers, particularly in relation to this text and other texts like it. Feminist critique warns against an explanation of the ritual, which by failing to expose it to searching critique, effectively normalizes it.[15]

13. Noth, *Numbers*, 50.

14. Mason, *Propaganda*, 107–8.

15. Bach, "Good." It is not my intention here to engage with the feminist critiques of this passage, not because I do not think such critiques significant but because the focus of my attention is on the question of literal and figural readings. My concern with the traditional Protestant reading stems at least in part from this ethical critique, and it is arguably the case that it is the Protestant way of reading the passage as a warning against adultery that has particularly nurtured feminist critiques of the *Sotah*, since the ritual can only be applied to wives. The typological reading of the passage that I offer could, not unfairly, be taken as an attempt to find a way to rehabilitate this passage. I am not unaware, though, that such a reading, at best, only mitigates the offence of this passage.

The *Sotah* in Ancient Hands

Alongside the "disastrous shrinkage" of the literal sense, we can also see in modern interpretations the use of allegorical interpretation in order to give the text significance in the present. There is some truth in the suggestion that the literal sense is what members of a reading community take to be the natural sense,[16] or, to put it another way, within a reading community it is very easy to lose the sense of the extent to which cherished readings and ways of reading are allegorical. Consequently, in order to establish that modern scholars resort to allegorical readings in attempting to supply the text with ongoing significance, it will be useful to view the *Sotah* within the history of its reception. By doing so we are made aware of other options for interpreting the ritual and what reading according to the literal sense might look like.

Within the Jewish interpretative tradition the *Sotah* received considerable attention from the rabbis and a whole mishnaic tractate is devoted to the subject. For them the ritual was no longer an active practice, and it is natural to assume that this was a consequence of the destruction of the Temple in AD 70. Rabbinic interpreters, however, dated the termination of the ritual to the same period of time, but suggest this was due to an increase in male adulterers or the increased openness of the immorality.[17] A literal mode of interpretation was followed, with a strong concern to describe how the ritual took place. Despite this, the "Sages have redefined the entire program."[18] The ritual was subordinated to a system of warnings and witnesses so that the husband cannot take action except where there is "well-established doubt" of his wife's fidelity but no witnesses have caught

16. Tanner offers a functional understanding of the plain sense where "the plain sense of a *scriptural* text in specific would consequently be what a participant in the community automatically or naturally takes a text to be saying on its face insofar as he or she has been socialized in a community's conventions for reading the text as scripture" (Tanner, "Theology," 63). Within its limits, such a functionally constrained definition has its advantages: it allows a clear distinction between the plain or literal sense and extended senses, it is inclusive of the many different understandings of the literal sense that have operated within Christian communities, and it rightly recognizes the role of the community in establishing the literal sense. Nevertheless, it does not provide critical leverage on the specific points at which different Christian groups have disagreed on their understanding of the literal sense, particularly, in the argument I am pursuing, where groups separated over the centuries have operated with different understandings of the literal sense of Numbers 5.

17. *m. Sotah.* 9:9; *t. Sotah* 14:2.

18. Neusner, *Rabbis,* 78.

her *in flagrante delicto*.[19] Creative readings of the interpretative gaps in the biblical text allow rabbinic interpreters to produce a reading of the ordeal that is both literal and of contemporary relevance. The result is somewhat unsatisfactory, though, for it is only in the gaps of the literal meaning that the contemporary significance appears.

The interpretation of the *Sotah* by the rabbis is fairly well known and has received a number of modern expositions; the case is otherwise with Christian interpretations where the *Sotah* has been interpreted in a number of different ways. An early interpretation of the *Sotah* is found in the *Protevangelium of James*, which describes the events leading up to the birth of Jesus. When Mary is discovered to be pregnant she and Joseph are compelled to undergo the ordeal.

The high priest said: "I will give you both to drink the water of the conviction of the Lord, and it will make manifest your sins before your eyes." And the high priest took it and gave it to Joseph to drink and sent him into the wilderness; and he came back whole. And he made Mary also drink, and sent her into the wilderness; and she also returned whole. And the people marvelled, because the water had not revealed any sin in them.[20]

This tradition also finds expression in middle Byzantine iconography of Mary.[21] In this tradition the literal interpretation of Num 5 is central, but its role is ultimately prophetic, resulting in the confirmation of the virgin birth of Jesus Christ. The purpose of Num 5, in the truest sense, would not be the discovery of the adulterous wife, but the confirmation of the purity of Mary. As a way of interpreting the *Sotah* it has attractions, for its prophetic understanding of the ritual depends upon a reading according to the literal sense. It does, however, depart from the literal sense for it requires that both Mary and Joseph be put to the test. This represents a subtle shift from the jealousy of the husband with marriage to concerns about pre-marital, or perhaps extra-marital, sex.

Medieval commentators explored the typological potential of the passage in a number of different ways, in which they related the ritual to the realities of Christ and the church. Bartlett summarizes this diversity: "the wronged husband is Christ or the Church, the adulterous woman the

19. Neusner, *Rabbis*, 79; b. *Sotah* 2a–3b.

20. *Prot. Jas.* 16:1–3. Translation from Hennecke, *New Testament Apocrypha I*, 370–88.

21. Weitzmann, *Fresco Cycle*, 48–50.

human soul, heretics, or the synagogue, the waters Scripture."[22] Alongside these typological interpretations, however, the medieval church grappled with the question of whether a literal reading of Num 5 justified the ordeals of fire and water commonly used from AD 800–1200.[23]

The ordeal seems to have originated with the Frankish tribes, but with the rise of the Carolingian Empire was incorporated into the general framework of medieval Christendom. As Christianity spread into northern and eastern Europe the practice of the ordeal naturally followed. During this period, it was known as the *iudicium Dei,* "the judgment of God," and was invoked for secret and pernicious crimes, such as adultery, sorcery, and heresy, when witnesses were lacking. Since the judgment of God was sought the medieval church was directly involved in its application. To be properly conducted a priest or bishop was needed.

During the heyday of the ordeal, opinion was divided about its use and Num 5 was discussed on both sides. Many assumed that the ordeal was a necessary judicial tool, and some defended it as scriptural. In a work opposing the attempt by Lothar II of Lotharingia to divorce his queen in AD 858, Hincmar, archbishop of Rheims, quoted Num 5 in defence of the ordeal. On the other hand, there was unease at the practice, and sometimes opposition, most notably from Agobard, archbishop of Lyons (AD 816–840), and Pope Stephen V (AD 885–91). In the eleventh and twelfth centuries AD ecclesiastical opposition to the practice was to increase climaxing in the rejection of the practice at the fourth Lateran Council (AD 1215). Two theological objections were raised against the ordeal. First, the ordeal was a human invention and, thus, uncanonical. Secondly, God's judgments are impenetrable. They cannot be harnessed by men, and any attempt to do so is to test God: "ordeal by hot iron or water is illicit because a miraculous effect is required from God" (Aquinas).[24] Yet how was the challenge of the existence of Num 5 in Scripture to be met? Bartlett notes,

> The critics of the ordeal eventually dealt with the Numbers passage by arguing that it was an exceptional concession. In the words of Peter Comestor, author of the standard text, the *Historia*

22. Bartlett, *Trial*, 84.

23. For the following account, see especially Bartlett, *Trial,* and the literature cited therein.

24. *Summa Theologica,* 2.2.95.8.

Scholastica, "this law was introduced because of the hardness of their hearts, just as the petition for divorce was allowed."[25]

With the exception of Num 5 removed, the silence of Scripture on the ordeal was compelling.

What characterizes Christian pre-modern exegesis of the *Sotah* is a literal reading of the text which sits alongside, or rather encompasses, figural readings of the text. Alternatively, we might say that the figural readings develop organically out of the literal reading. That is, because the subject matter of the literal reading is requisitioned by the divine author for his purposes, it is suited for the task of representing the realities of Christ and the church. Thus, these allegorical readings see the *Sotah* within the wider context of the witness of Scripture so that the text speaks of the climax of salvation. These readings do not entail the loss of the literal sense, since they rely on its detail, but rather the development and expansion of the literal sense within the whole canon.

The *Sotah* in Modern Hands

When we turn to the modern period we do not find the disappearance of allegorical readings, despite protestations to the contrary. Indeed, some form of figural reading is going to be necessary if the text is going to be valued as Holy Scripture that speaks to the contemporary church.

By far the most common strategy among modern interpreters is to discern in Num 5 an affirmation of the importance of marital fidelity and an emphatic disapproval of adultery. A few examples will suffice. In a commentary series aimed at the interested evangelical reader, Gordon Wenham concludes his discussion of the *Sotah* with the following summary:

> It was designed to reassure suspicious husbands that, even if they had no proof themselves of their wives' infidelity, God would assuredly punish the guilty and demonstrate the innocence of the faithful (cf. vv. 27–28, 31). It was also a graphic and dramatic representation of the importance of purity in marriage; and as every human marriage is an image of the relationship between God and his people, it also reminds us of the faithfulness God requires in his servants.[26]

25. Bartlett, *Trial*, 84.
26. Wenham, *Numbers*, 85.

The move from descriptive prose to application is clear as Wenham moves from past to present tense: "it was" becomes "is" and "reminds." Numbers 5 instructs the modern reader about faithfulness and marital purity. Jacob Milgrom finds a similar message here. The implication is clear: "This kind of defilement is no less offensive to God and, if not punished, will lead to his abandonment of Israel."[27] A detailed excursus provides further substantiation as the *Sotah* legislation is placed in the wider context of attitudes to adultery in the Old Testament and the ancient Near East.[28] In his Word Biblical Commentary Philip Budd writes,

> Theologically the section bears further witness to the moral seriousness of the priestly literature. Marital deceit is a matter of such seriousness that the truth must be discovered . . . Modern practice of the ordeal would obviously be indefensible, but a modern moral seriousness, aiming for healthy relationships, has to recognize the destructive effect of suspicion, and find means to allay and eliminate it.[29]

This is a reading of the text that moves to a higher level of abstraction, but it is still belongs recognizably to the same family of readings.

This way of reading the *Sotah* has a long heritage within the Protestant tradition. Calvin, for example, writes,

> By this rite, therefore, God proclaims Himself the guardian and avenger of conjugal fidelity; and hence it appears how acceptable a sacrifice in His sight is the chastity of married women, of which He condescends to profess Himself the guardian.[30]

27. Milgrom, *Numbers*, 351.

28. Milgrom, *Numbers*, 348–50.

29. Budd, *Numbers*, 66, 67.

30. Calvin, *Four Last Books of Moses*, 3:87. Unfortunately this tradition of interpretation has not always been as distinguished as it might have been. In an ominous anticipation of some Christian responses to the modern experience of AIDS, Matthew Henry connects the effect of the bitter waters on the woman with the syphilis epidemics that plagued Europe in the sixteenth and seventeenth centuries,

> [It is] a disease perhaps not much unlike that which in these latter ages the avenging hand of a righteous God has made the scourge of uncleanness, and with which whores and whoremongers infect, and plague, and ruin one another, since they escape punishment from men. (Henry, *Commentary*, on Num 5.11–31)

Henry cannot avoid an easy addressing of God's immanent judgment in the world.

Despite its heritage, we should observe that this interpretation is not straightforwardly a literal reading of the text, though undoubtedly many take it as such. Even without knowledge of the history of the ordeal in medieval Europe, which could make better claim to be a literal reading, Budd's comments about the indefensibility of a modern practice of the *Sotah* exposes the fact that there is a way of reading the story *literally* that most modern readers would not wish to contemplate. Reading the *Sotah* as a warning about adultery is, in the words of the medieval rhyme, *moralis quid agas*, a reading according to the moral sense of the text, a reading that teaches us how to live.

The strength of such an interpretation is its reading within the context of the Mosaic law. Calvin famously organized his interpretation of the law according to the Ten Commandments, and the *Sotah* was naturally discussed within the context of the seventh commandment. The problem with this way of interpreting the *Sotah*—besides the vulnerability to feminist critique because of the unbalanced applicability of the rite—is that it reads the text in an abstract manner. Arguably, this leads to a loss of the literal such that the passage becomes nothing more than a Jülicherian parable with one point: do not commit adultery. But not only does the text not do this (the prohibition of adultery is found elsewhere), it is also a reification of the passage.

Another interpretation is offered by the Jewish interpreters Milgrom and Brichto, who discern in Num 5 the priestly appropriation of a pagan ritual ordeal in order to liberate the suspected adulteress from a vengeful husband. According to Milgrom, an originally magical ritual has been interpreted within the context of Yahwistic theology. Without witnesses the husband's suspicions cannot be resolved judicially. The *Sotah* ritual hands over the judgment to God and protects the accused woman from the actions of the lynch mob.

> In sum, the biblical law of the suspected adulteress provides a unique example of how the priestly legislators made use of a pagan ordeal in order to protect a suspected but unproved adulteress from the vengeance of an irate husband or community by mandating that God will decide her case.[31]

Brichto's interpretation is more rationalistic. Although the ritual's effectiveness is now attributed to God in the biblical text, the biblical writers are

31. Milgrom, *Numbers*, 354.

operating with an understanding of the potential of psychosomatic effects on the guilty. The likelihood of an innocent woman suffering any ill-effect from drinking the water is negligible and for a guilty woman slight. The intention of the ritual, according to Brichto, was to redress the patriarchal bias in society. Unsubstantiated accusations would have to be brought to the temple where an almost ineffective ritual would silence them.[32]

The interpretations offered by Milgrom and Brichto evidence a concern with the feminist critique and the possibility that Israel's scriptures authorize a *magic* ritual. Nevertheless, as was the case with the adultery interpretation, they cannot be understood as a reading according to the literal sense of the text. Indeed, the novelty of their reading is defended by making a disjunction between what the ritual explicitly concerns (the determination of whether or not the accused is an adulteress) and what it actually effects (the protection of vulnerable women). Interpreted thus, the text teaches that judgment for secret sins rests with God,[33] or that there should be equality between men and women. Each of these could be seen as *quid credas allegoria*, the allegorical sense that teaches us what to believe. On the other hand, since both Milgrom and Brichto hold that the ritual is a non-magical development from a magical ritual we could also hold that we have here *quo tendas anagogia*, an anagogical interpretation showing us our future destiny in a rational world where the only divine power is Israel's God. Yet, these figural means of interpretation are not a development or extension of the literal sense but the negation of it. They only make sense if the ritual does not achieve what the text *literally* says it achieves.

The point of these modern examples is to show the presence of figural modes of interpretation, despite assumptions that what is being ventured are literal readings of the Old Testament text. That they are readings according to the allegorical, moral, or analogical sense makes them no worse for it, but we should not hesitate to identify them for what they are. The point is merely a descriptive one, and not a prescriptive one. But beyond that there is an unconscious irony about these interpretations since, although they are viewed as literal readings, they actually entail the undermining of the literal sense.[34] The figural interpretations do not flow organically from

32. Brichto, "Case." Cf. Driver, "Two Problems."

33. This makes for a rather interesting comparison to medieval Christian concerns about the judgment of God.

34. Von Rad makes a very similar accusation against the *Religionsgeschichte* of his day in his attempt to rehabilitate a certain form of typological exegesis. In his view the

the literal reading, but are a contraction of the literal sense or a reading against it. In order for these readings to establish themselves they need to reify the text or reverse its plain sense. Such allegorizing is a natural counterpart of the "disastrous shrinkage" of the literal sense.

Reconsidering the Case of the *Sotah*

Is it possible to read the *Sotah* according to the literal sense but moving to figural interpretations in a way that is not arbitrary or negates the literal sense? I want to argue that there are a number of features in Num 5 that suggest the text is to be read figurally, speaking of the relationship between YHWH and Israel and, within the context of a Christian two testament canon, between God and the church. To read in such a way does not mean losing the specificity of the text. In fact, certain details in the text suggest the appropriateness of such a reading. It will mean a reading according to the literal sense within the larger context of Old and, ultimately, New Testaments.

My suggested figural reading of the passage is to find here a description of the relationship between YHWH and Israel in the wilderness, where YHWH is the jealous husband and Israel, the wife suspected of unfaithfulness. The wilderness is, in the Pentateuch's portrayal, a time when Israel is probed in a most searching manner in order to ascertain her faithfulness to YHWH (Exod 15:25–26; 16:4–5; Deut 8:2–5). This probing takes place particularly through the provision miracles, in which Israel's response to the food and drink that YHWH provides reveals her attitude to YHWH and his commandments (Exod 15–17; Num 11, 20). In the testing stories that follow the Sinai revelation this attitude can result in death or life. Three aspects of Numbers 5 suggest such a figural reading.

First, the description of the woman at the beginning of the law has a number of terms which are distinctive or used in unusual ways. The

---

concern with religion was a reification that meant that "an entire dimension the fullness of its [the Old Testament's] witness to history is excluded" (von Rad, "Typological Interpretation," 24). For von Rad, *Religionsgeschichte*, with its exclusive concern with the spiritual and intellectual and its indifference to the historical events of Israel's existence, aligns not only with non-historical forms of analogy, but specifically with allegorical interpretation (which von Rad viewed negatively as a form of dehistoricizing). Thus, *Religionsgeschichte* despite its professed interest in history actually results in a dehistoricizing of the biblical text. Theological exegesis, though accused of a preoccupation with universal timeless values, is actually more concerned than *Religionsgeschichte* with the particularity of Israel's history.

accusation against the wife is that she has gone "astray," for which the rare word *śāṭah* is used. Although the term is used of the ways of the adulteress in Prov 7:25, its use there and in 4:15 is broader than just adultery. It is to turn away from the paths of righteousness and wisdom. This is coupled with a description of the wife as "unfaithful" (*ma'al*) to her husband in Num 5:12. *Ma'al* undoubtedly functions in part as a catchword that links the *Sotah* to the preceding pericope about the *'asham* (vv. 5–10). It is, however, an unusual word since it is used of offences against YHWH, including idolatry (Lev 26:40; Num 31:16), rather than against other humans.[35] In other words, the offence, which the wife is suspected of committing, appears to be not simply a case of suspected adultery.

Second, we may ponder the significance of the water. As we have seen, the exact significance of *mê hammārim* is unclear. Nevertheless, whether we understand a relationship to *marah* "to be rebellious, contentious" or *marar* "to be bitter," they are somewhat suggestive of stories about water provision during Israel's wilderness experience. The waters of Marah are so called because they were bitter (Exod 15:23). In the final form of the Pentateuch the Marah incident is a paradigm for Israel's experience of being tested in the wilderness (15:25b–26). It has often been suggested that there is a relationship between the bitter waters in Num 5 and the waters that Moses made the Israelites drink after the sin of the Golden Calf. Although Moses washed the dust of the Calf in the water which he made the Israelites drink, there are no significant verbal parallels between the two passages. In addition, it has been observed that Exod 32 "is not concerned with the ascertainment but with the eradication of guilt."[36]

Third, we should give attention to the location of the *Sotah* in its immediate context. The *Sotah* is part of a collection of laws in Num 5–6. Within this material there are two large pieces of legislation, the Nazirite

35. The possible typological significance is noted by Douglas, *Wilderness*, 161. Milgrom notes, "this is the only time that the term *ma'al* is used outside the sacred sphere of sancta and oath violations, where the object of *ma'al* is invariably the Deity" (Milgrom, *Numbers*, 37).

36. Krasovec, *Reward*, 103. Nevertheless, many ancient interpreters understood the water to bring death to those guilty of worshipping the calf, whilst the innocent were preserved alive. Amongst them, Ephrem the Syrian writes, "Moses pulverized the calf and made them drink it in the waters of testing, so that all who had lived to worship the calf would die by drinking it." The connection with the rite for the suspected wife is explicit, for the term "the water of testing" is drawn from Num 5 rather than Exod 32 (noted by E. Beck in Ephrem the Syrian, *Domino Nostro*, 6 n. 3).

and the *Sotah*. The two portrayals appear to be a contrasting pair, as was noticed as early as the medieval Jewish scholar Ramban.[37] There are a number of similarities: both the wife and the Nazirite are brought by others to the sanctuary (5:15; 6:13); the state of their hair has symbolic significance for both (5:18; 6:5); each makes a vow or oath (5:19–21; 6:2); each has offerings placed in their hands (5:18; 6:19); each law has a concluding colophon: "This is the law of . . ." (5:29; 6:21). We might also observe that the water of bitterness is used in the rite of the women suspected of unfaithfulness (5:18) and the water of cleansing is used if the Nazirite is defiled by a corpse (6:9; cf. Num 19). We might call this pair of portrayals a diptych. On first appearances it might appear that we have a positive and a negative portrait. Yet, the wife is only suspected of adultery and the Nazirite offers a sin offering at the completion of his vow. Both members of the diptych combine sin and non-sin, though the emphasis differs in each portrait.

The instructions concerning Nazirites and the *Sotah* form, with other instructions, a collection within a narrative context. As such they stand outside the numerous Pentateuchal legal collections. Within the book of Numbers this is not unusual, the narrative framework is frequently interspersed with legal material (Num 5–6, 15, 18–19, 27–30, 35–36). In some cases the logic behind the placement of these legal sections can be discerned (e.g. Num 27, 35), but on other occasions it is far from clear (e.g. Num 15). In the case of Num 5–6 the narrative context concerns the preparations of the Israelite community to depart from Sinai and journey through the wilderness towards the Promised Land. Thus, the *Sotah* and the Nazirite are placed here prior to the Israelites' departure from Sinai in order to set before the Israelites two possible responses to YHWH. The *Sotah* represents an Israel with the potential to fall short of its status as YHWH's partner. Testing in the wilderness reveals either a faithful or unfaithful Israel with life or death the result. The Nazirite presents an ideal Israel, avoiding all defilement, faithfully fulfilling her vow.

Conclusion: The *Sotah*—Literal and Figural

The figural interpretation develops organically from a literal reading. Indeed, it is encompassed in a literal reading because the figural interpretation is a reading within the wider canonical context. Such a reading does

37. For a recent comparison, see Diamond, "Israelite Self-Offering."

not entail the negation of the literal reading as was the case with those interpretations that find in Num 5 merely a warning against adultery or a psychosomatic trick. This is true even if we question whether Num 5 was ever intended to result in a *literal* application. A figural reading without a literal application can easily be recognized as a literal reading on analogy with the use of metaphors. To deny a literal application does not undo the literal reading since the figural reading relies on the details of the *Sotah* and does not abstract a moral message from it or undercut by reading against the grain. Thus, we find ourselves in the paradoxical position that the figural reading is the truly literal reading, and the literal readings are not.

Bibliography

Bach, Alice. "Good to the Last Drop: Viewing the *Sotah* (Numbers 5.11–31) as the Glass Half Empty and Wondering How to View it Half Full." In *The New Literary Criticism and the Hebrew Bible*, edited by J. Cheryl Exum and David J. A. Clines, 26–54. JSOTSup, 143. Sheffield: JSOT Press, 1993.

Bartlett, R., *Trial by Fire and Water: The Medieval Judicial Ordeal.* Oxford: Clarendon, 1986.

Brichto, H. C. "The Case of the atoS and a Reconsideration of Biblical 'Law.'" *HUCA* 46 (1975) 55–70.

Budd, Philip J. *Numbers.* WBC 5. Waco: Word, 1984.

Calvin, John, *The Four Last Books of Moses Arranged in the Form of a Harmony.* Translated by Charles William Bingham. Grand Rapids: Baker, 1993

Davies, Eryl W. *Numbers.* NCB. Grand Rapids: Eerdmans, 1995.

Diamond, E. "An Israelite Self-Offering in the Priestly Code: A New Perspective on the Nazirite." *JQR* 88 (1997) 1–18.

Douglas, Mary. *In the Wilderness: The Doctrine of Defilement in the Book of Numbers.* JSOTSup 158. Sheffield: JSOT Press, 1993.

Driver, Godfrey R. "Two Problems in the Old Testament Examined in the Light of Assyriology." *Syria* 33 (1956) 70–78.

Ephrem the Syrian. *Des Heiligen Ephraem des Syrers Sermo de Domino Nostro.* CSCO 271. Louvain: Secrétariat du CorpusSCO, 1966.

Fishbane, Michael. "Accusations of Adultery: A Study of Law and Scribal Practice in Numbers 5:11–31." *HUCA* 45 (1974) 25–45.

Frei, Hans W. *The Eclipse of Biblical Narrative: A Study in Eighteenth and Nineteenth Century Hermeneutics.* New Haven: Yale University Press, 1974.

Gray, George Buchanan. *Numbers.* ICC. Edinburgh: T. & T. Clark, 1965.

Hennecke, E. *New Testament Apocrypha I.* London: SCM, 1963.

Henry, Matthew, *Commentary on the Whole Bible.* Vol. 1: *Genesis to Joshua*, New York: Revell, 1935.

Krasovec, Joze. *Reward, Punishment, and Forgiveness: The Thinking and Beliefs of Ancient Israel in the Light of Greek and Modern Views.* VTSup 78. Leiden: Brill, 1999.

Mason, Rex. *Propaganda and Subversion in the Old Testament*. London: SPCK, 1997.

Milgrom, Jacob. "The Case of the Suspected Adulteress, Numbers 5:11–31: Redaction and Meaning." In *The Creation of Sacred Literature: Composition and Redaction of the Biblical Text*, edited by R. E. Friedman, 69–75. Berkeley: University of California Press, 1981.

———. *Numbers*. Jewish Publication Society Torah Commentary. Philadelphia: Jewish Publication Society, 1990.

Neusner, Jacob. *How the Rabbis Liberated Women*. South Florida Studies in the History of Judaism 191. Atlanta: Scholars, 1998.

Noth, Martin. *Numbers*. OTL. London: SCM, 1968.

———. *Die vierte Buch Mose: Numeri*. ATD. Göttingen: Vandenhoeck & Ruprecht, 1966.

Rad, Gerhard von. "Typological Interpretation of the Old Testament." In *Essays on Old Testament Hermeneutics*, edited by Claus Westermann, 17–39. Atlanta: John Knox, 1963.

Sasson, Jack M. "Numbers 5 and the 'Waters of Judgement.'" *BZ* 16 (1972) 249–51.

Seitz, Christopher R. *Figured Out: Typology and Providence in Christian Scripture*. Louisville: Westminster John Knox, 2001.

Stade, B. "Beiträge zur Pentateuchkritik." *ZAW* 15 (1895) 157–78.

Tanner, Kathryn E. "Theology and Plain Sense." In *Scriptural Authority and Narrative Interpretation*, edited by Garrett Green, 59–78. Philadelphia: Fortress, 1987.

Weitzmann, K. *The Fresco Cycle of S. Maria di Castelseprio*. Princeton: Princeton University Press, 1951.

Wenham, Gordon. *Numbers*. TOTC. Leicester: IVP, 1981.

Williams, Rowan. "The Discipline of Scripture." In *On Christian Theology*, 44–59. Oxford: Blackwell, 2000.

6

Moses and Joshua

Servants of the Lord as Purveyors of the Word

Frank Anthony Spina

MOSES CERTAINLY AND JOSHUA ARGUABLY ARE AMONG THE MOST prominent of biblical characters. After all, Moses dominates all but the first (Genesis) of the five books of the Torah/Pentateuch (Exodus—Deuteronomy), a biblical section that sets the stage for everything that follows.[1] As for Joshua, he is Moses' successor and consequently the main figure in the story in which the promise of the land YHWH made to the ancestors is fulfilled (Joshua). Without question, the events in which these two stalwarts are involved are among the most noteworthy and strategic in all of the biblical material. Absent the events in which these two particular characters play such key roles, the biblical epic would be truncated beyond recognition. They served their God with ardor and distinction.

The Prominence of Moses and Joshua

As though it were not enough for Moses to be the recipient of a most special revelation (Exod 3:1—4:17),[2] to speak for YHWH from the time of the burning bush incident to when Israel was poised on the "verge of Jordan" (see Exod 3:13–18; 4:10–16),[3] to announce the plagues in YHWH's behalf (Exod 7–12), consecrate the first born (Exod 13:1–2), receive and pass on

---

1. Ever since scholars began to emphasize the importance of canonical shaping, they have called attention to the strategic role of Torah. See Brevard S. Childs, *Introduction*, 131–32; Sanders, *Torah and Canon*.

2. See the treatment of this important text by Christopher Seitz, "The Call of Moses," 145–61.

3. *YHWH* speaks directly to the people only in Exod 20:1–17. See Exod 20:18–19.

65

instructions for the perpetual celebration of Passover (Exod 12:1–27; 13:3–10), preside over the miracle at the sea and sing (with the people) a great hymn of praise to YHWH (Exod 14:1–15:21), lead the people through the wilderness with all the *magnalia dei* associated with that epochal journey (e.g., Exod 15:22–27; 16:1–36; 17:1–7), and, finally, to play a critical role in God's covenant making with Israel (Exod 20:21–Num 10), he is additionally singled out as the sole Israelite who speaks with YHWH "face to face" (Exod 33:7–11; v. 11: *pānîm 'el-pānîm*; see 34:29–35), making him the quintessential Israelite prophet (Deut 34:10–11; see 18:15–22). It is difficult to imagine a more impressive resumé.

Compared to Moses, Joshua, not surprisingly, gets a little less coverage. Still, he also is depicted in exemplary terms, including his being presented eventually as a "second Moses." To be sure, early on Joshua primarily receives and carries out instructions from Moses (e.g., Exod 17:9, 10, 13; Num 32:28 [along with Eleazar]; 34:17 [along with Eleazar]). But mostly he is depicted as singular. Joshua alone is called Moses' "minister" (*mᵉšārēt*; Exod 24:13; 33:11; Num 11:28; see Josh 1:1). Then again, he is with Moses during special encounters with YHWH (Exod 24:12–13; 32:17). We are even informed in the passage about God's speaking uniquely to Moses that Joshua did not depart from the "tent" (of meeting) when his mentor departed for the Israelite camp (Exod 33:11). This tent, as is well known, was where the pillar of cloud would descend and YHWH would speak to Moses (Exod 33:7–9; see 33:1–10). Joshua is moreover one of the Israelites selected to spy on the divinely promised land (Num 13:16). More importantly, he and Caleb are the only two spies who challenged the despairing report of their confreres (Num 13:27–29, 31–33; 14:6–9), none of whom believed that YHWH could make good on the promise to deliver the land, given its formidable inhabitants. As a result, only Joshua and Caleb, who "have wholly followed the Lord,"[4] are spared the judgment visited upon the pessimistic spies and those Israelites who faithlessly accepted their gloomy appraisal (Num 14:30, 38; 26:65; 32:12). Joshua is in time commissioned as Moses' successor so that, in Moses' own words, "the congregation of YHWH may not be as sheep which have no shepherd" (Num 27:18–22). In Moses' last address to Israel, he describes Joshua's new role with God's people (Deut 1:38; 3:21, 28). Shortly before his death, Moses charges and encourages Joshua in his new position,

---

4. Translations follow the RSV except for replacing "the LORD" with the Tetragrammaton *YHWH*. I note where there are other exceptions.

whereupon he is personally commissioned by YHWH (Deut 31:3, 7, 14, 23; 34:9). Virtually the only mildly negative portrayal of Joshua occurs when he asks Moses to forbid Eldad and Medad from prophesying, a request whose rationale Moses rejects (Num 11:28).[5]

Joshua plays his most decisive role in the book that bears his name. His execution of "the battle of Jericho" most readily comes to mind (Josh 6), but other of his feats are similarly remarkable. He circumcised an entire generation to conform to Torah's stipulations, thereby removing the "reproach of Egypt" (Josh 5:2–9), presided over an Israel who celebrated Passover in the land of promise and for the first time began to eat the produce of the land rather than manna (Josh 5:10–12), rooted out an Israelite evildoer by finding and condemning Achan, thus averting Israel's being "proscribed" or "put to the ban" (RSV: "become a thing for destruction"; Josh 7:1–26; see v. 12), held up his javelin during the battle of Ai until victory was assured (Josh 8:18, 26), pled successfully to God for the sun and moon to stand still (Josh 10:12–14), and led Israel at a time when it was adjudged a faithful generation for serving YHWH all its days (Josh 24:31).

As intimated above, Joshua is also presented in the guise of a "second Moses."[6] After receiving at the outset encouragement and instruction from YHWH, and in turn commanding and encouraging Israel, the people respond, "Just as we obeyed Moses in all things, so we will obey you; only may YHWH your God be with you, *as he was with Moses*" (Josh 1:16–17; see also 1:2–9, 10–15; italics mine). YHWH then, after the Rahab incident (Josh 2), exalts Joshua and promises to be with him *as he was with Moses* (Josh 3:7, italics mine). When Joshua leads the people in a miraculous crossing of the Jordan, his action parallels that of Moses' at the *Yam Sûp* (Josh 3:8–17).[7] His position as a "second Moses" is underscored after

5. Joshua's sending of the spies in the Rahab incident (Josh 2:1) is perhaps to be construed in somewhat negative terms. That is, it is unclear why Joshua felt the need to send spies in the first place since what *YHWH* had told him about the prospect of taking over the land had been so unequivocal (Josh 1:2–5). Rahab's agreement with the spies led to Israel's violation of the "rules of engagement" regarding the inhabitants of the land of promise (Deut 20:16–18). Likewise, though *YHWH*'s response to Achan's/Israel's violation of the "ban" (Josh 7:1) does not single out Joshua for reprimand, presumably he is included as part of Israel (Josh 7:10–15). See Spina, "Rahab and Achan," in *The Faith of the Outsider*, 52–71.

6. See Christoph Barth, "Moses, Knecht Gottes," 79.

7. In addition to the thematic connections between the two divinely-aided crossings, in both instances the waters stood in a "heap" (*nēd*). See Exod 15:8; Josh 3:13. In Josh 4:23, Joshua makes explicit mention of the *Yam Sûp* crossing.

the crossing as well: "On that day YHWH exalted Joshua in the sight of all Israel; and they stood in awe of him, *as they had stood in awe of Moses*, all the days of his life" (Josh 4:14; italics mine). Though Joshua does not have a "burning bush" episode, he is confronted by a "man" (*'îš*) with his sword drawn who identifies himself as "commander of YHWH's army" (*śar-ṣᵉbā'-YHWH*) and demands that the Israelite leader remove his shoes because of the holy ground on which he is standing (Josh 5:13–15).[8] Perhaps Joshua's holding up his javelin during the battle of Ai is meant to resemble what Moses (and later Aaron and Hur) did when he held up his hands during the Amelekite battle (Exod 17:8–13; see Josh 8:18, 26). Joshua does not quite attain Moses' "rank," but his efforts as a "second Moses" are nevertheless laudatory.

Serving YHWH

Given this positive depiction, it should be a foregone conclusion that Moses and Joshua would be called "servants of YHWH." It virtually goes without saying that "serving" YHWH or being YHWH's "servant," whether ap-plied to Israel as a whole or to individual Israelites, is among the most fa-miliar ways in the biblical tradition for designating appropriate obedience and response to the deity.[9] If in a social, economic, or political context a servant (Hebrew: *'ebed*) is a person who belongs to or does the bidding of another person or institution, then in the religious realm a "servant of YHWH" is a person or community who belongs to and does the bidding of Israel's God. The difference is that being God's "servant"—or "slave," for the terms are synonymous, differentiated only by context—is not a function of necessity or force but of covenant devotion and obligation based on YHWH's prior gracious actions toward the elect community.[10]

Indicative of the pervasive use of this concept, when YHWH is the speaker the following are identified as the deity's servants (= "My servant"): Abraham, Moses, Caleb, David, Isaiah, the unnamed Isaianic servant, Nebuchadrezzar/Nebuchadnezzar, Zerubbabel, the Branch, Job,

---

8. See the treatment of this mysterious figure by Davis, "The Poetics of Generosity," 14–15. See also Davis' citation of Rutledge, "What the Angel Said," 12. My thanks to Ellen Davis for allowing me to see a pre-publication copy of her essay.

9. See Lindhagen, The Servant Motif; Riesener; Der Stamm עבד; Ringgren, "עבד 'Abad"; Zimmerli and Jeremias, The Servant of God.

10. See Zimmerli and Jeremias, The Servant of God, 13.

Eliakim, and Israel itself.[11] On occasion, YHWH designates a group of specialized personnel or people in general as "my servants." First Kings 9:7 contains references to both. In that passage, a prophet speaking in YHWH's behalf declares to Jehu, ". . . you shall strike down the house of Ahab your master, that I may avenge on Jezebel the blood of *my servants the prophets*, and the blood of *all the servants of the Lord*" (italics mine).[12] Throughout the biblical material individuals or Israel are either referred to as YHWH's servants or are said to serve the deity.

In this light, characterizing either Moses or Joshua as YHWH's servant along with other biblical worthies seems unremarkable. For that reason, while their service to God presumably enhances their stellar reputations to a degree, it does not in and of itself require that they should be thought of as unique. Other attributes or accomplishments would have to stand out before regarding their service as different *in kind* from other of God's servants. Serving YHWH is fundamentally an expectation for all Israelites.

Few passages express more directly how crucial it is for all Israel to serve YHWH than Joshua's final address to Israel. After rehearsing YHWH's mighty actions in Israel's behalf (Josh 24:1–13), Joshua commands the people to "fear" and "serve" (*wᵉ'ibᵉdû*) their God, in this instance by rejecting all other deities. Regardless of whom Israel finally decides to serve (*la'ᵃbōd*), Joshua is adamant that "as for me and my house, we will serve (*na'ᵃbōd*) YHWH" (Josh 24:14–15). Notwithstanding the prompt positive response of the people to Joshua's challenge, presumably indicating that they are willing to eschew serving other gods (Josh 24:16–17: *la'ᵃbōd 'ᵉlōhîm 'ᵃḥērîm*) and commit to serving YHWH exclusively (Josh

---

11. Abraham (Gen 26:24); Moses (Num 12:7, 8; Josh 1:2, 7; 2 Kgs 21:8; Mal 3:22); Caleb (Num 14:24); David (2 Sam 3:13; 7:5, 8; 1 Kgs 11:13, 32, 34, 36, 38; 14:8; 2 Kgs 19:34; 20:6; Isa 37:35; 41:8; Jer 33:21, 22, 26; Ezek 34:23, 24; 37:24, 25; Psalm 89:4, 21; 1 Chr 17:4, 7); Isaiah (Isa 20:3); Israel [or synonyms] (Lev 25:42, 55; Isa 41:8, 9; 43:10; 44:1, 2, 21; 45:4; 49:3; 65:8, 9, 13, 14; Jer 30:10; 46:27, 28; Ezek 28:25; 37:25); Unnamed Servant of Isaiah (Isa 42:1, 19; 52:13; 53:11); Nebuchadrezzar/Nebuchadnezzar (Jer 25:9; 27:6; 43:10); Zerubbabel (Hag 2:23); the Branch (Zech 3:8); Job (Job 1:8; 2:3; 42:7, 8); Eliakim (Isa 22:20).

12. Other references to the prophets collectively are: 2 Kgs 17:13; Jer 7:25; 26:5; 29:19; 35:15; 44:4; Ezek 38:17; Zech 1:6. See Mowinckel's comment: "As a title of honour, and as an expression of an active mission, the 'Servant of Yahweh' is applied in the Old Testament . . . first and foremost to the prophets." Mowinckel, *He That Cometh*, 225. Mowinckel does not, however, distinguish between the term *'ebed* generally and the actual phrase *'ebed* YHWH. References to "the servants of YHWH," with the plural noun in construct with the following proper noun are: 2 Kgs 9:7; 10:23; Isa 54:17; Pss 113:1; 134:1; 135:1.

24:18: *gam-'**nahnû na'**bōd 'et-YHWH*), he immediately intuits that they do not truly understand the gravity of what he is asking of them. Thus, he calls them up short by denying their ability to serve (Josh 24:19: *lō' tûk**lû la'**bōd 'et-YHWH*) and warns of the dire consequences of their failure to realize that YHWH is a "jealous" God whose judgment will be severe if foreign gods are served instead of or even along with the Israelite deity (Josh 24:19–20: *kî ta'**z**bû 'et-YHWH wa'**badtem '**lōhê nēkār*). In a second response, after having heard this warning and apparently having now comprehended more fully what Joshua was demanding, the people pledge with an unambiguous oath—complete with "witnessing against yourselves"—by declaring with a double assertion: (1) "No! We will serve (Josh 24:21: *na'**bōd*) YHWH"; and, (2) "YHWH our God we will serve (Josh 24:24: *na'**bōd*), and his voice we will obey" (Josh 24:19–28). At this juncture in Israel's life, serving YHWH is put forward as the *sine qua non* of Israel's stance before God.

In sum, because the concept of serving YHWH or being called one of YHWH's servants is so widespread, and because this idea is so central to the essential theological outlook of the Old Testament, as the previous passage in Joshua illustrates, the fact that Moses and Joshua also served YHWH or are called YHWH's servants, in and of itself does little more than allow them to be considered along with all other faithful Israelites who appropriately serve the God who elected them. As good Israelites, what else would they do? To ask the question is to answer it.

'ebed YHWH as a Technical Term

Notwithstanding that Moses and Joshua serve YHWH in a manner commensurate with other biblical characters or with Israel as a whole, it may fairly be asked whether there are any reasons for positing that either Moses as "the servant of YHWH" or Joshua as "the servant of YHWH" are deserving of any special attention? Put more sharply, is there evidence that when *'ebed YHWH* is applied to Moses and Joshua the phrase functions as something other than a standard way of signaling appropriate religious behavior? Might *'ebed YHWH* evoke something more substantial, or even be construed as a technical term of sorts? As a corollary, if it is so used, does its meaning go beyond the assorted nuances normally associated with serving YHWH as a general matter of religious deportment?

The answers to these questions, in my judgment, are to be affirmative. As I hope to demonstrate, *'ebed YHWH* is used in relationship to Moses and Joshua precisely to underscore a specific aspect of their otherwise normal service to God. Regardless of all that they do generally to serve their deity, the *'ebed YHWH* nomenclature, its use and its placement, is designed to feature a distinctive form of their service.[13] As well, I shall attempt to show that the use of the *'ebed YHWH* language in the supposed Deuteronomistic History, most especially and predominantly in the Book of Joshua, is put into even bolder relief in the final canonical shaping of the material.[14] That final form presents the first major section, the Torah, as a Pentateuch and not as a Tetrateuch (or Hexateuch). When the canonical process, regardless of the prior shape of the received traditions, eventuated in an arrangement such that Deuteronomy was the last book of a pentateuchal Torah instead of the first book of what became the canonical Former Prophets, this had the effect of elevating a basic theological perspective regarding Moses and Joshua that had to do with the particular service they rendered to YHWH and by extension to Israel.[15]

13. It is conceivably the case that Isaiah's "servant" is also to be understood as having a specialized relationship to *YHWH* and Israel (though certainly distinct from that of Moses and Joshua). At the same time, only once is the phrase *'ebed YHWH* used in all the well-known servant passages.

14. I use the adjective "supposed" to modify "Deuteronomisitic History" to indicate the ongoing controversy regarding Martin Noth's original thesis. Variations on Noth's proposal continue to appear. In addition, the maturation of the variety of literary approaches to biblical material at least requires rethinking whether the presence of contradiction, tension, ambiguity, differences of outlook between implied narrators and characters, alteration of vocabulary, narrative gaps, and the like, are necessarily always best explained by the postulation of disparit discrete sources. Might these and other phenomena reflect a more "artful" process—at the redactional if not the composition level—behind the present canonical text? See Martin Noth, *Überlieferungsgeschichtliche Studien: die sammelnden und bearbeitenden Geschichtswerke im Alten Testament.* See also Noth, *The Deuteronomistic History.* See the recent discussion by K. L. Noll, "Deuteronomistic History or Deuteronomic Debate? (A Thought Experiement)," 311–45. Noll's treatment and voluminous bibliography are extremely helpful. At the same time, he seems to see biblical material in a most brittle and wooden manner in that virtually nothing that might be seen as "artful" or "creative" is ever conceded to the text. Where a different source *can* be posited it seems it *must* be posited. I agree with him that much of this material is "conversational" in the sense that there is no single, simplistic Deuteronomistic ideal against which equally univocal ideas are clumsily juxtaposed as antitheses. But I question his extreme atomizing of the text. In the context of this debate, see Vogt, *Deuteronomic Theology and the Significance of Torah.* In any case, whether the Deuteronomistic History hypothesis or one of its several permutations prevails, or is eventually discarded, is finally immaterial to the thesis put forward here.

15. On the importance of the Torah as a Pentateuch rather than a Tetrateuch or

The Occurrences of the *'ebed YHWH* Terminology

At the outset, the most important observation to make about *'ebed YHWH*'s potential use as a functional technical term is how seldom the full term— singular noun in construct relationship with the proper noun YHWH—is actually found in the Old Testament, especially given how widespread the idea of serving YHWH is. The specific phrase *'ebed YHWH* is found a scant twenty-three times in all of the Old Testament.[16] Even more telling than its relatively few uses, however, is the manner in which the term is employed, along with the pattern that obtains in its use. Among all named biblical characters, it turns out that only Moses, Joshua, and David are ever identified with the full title "the servant of YHWH." David is identified in this way in two Psalm titles (Pss 18:1; 36:1). Other than that, only Moses and Joshua are assigned this title. Of these occurrences, Joshua is accorded the title, like David, but twice (Josh 24:29; Judg 2:8). As for unnamed characters, the Isaianic servant is once and only once called *'ebed YHWH* (Isa 42:19; see n. 12). Equally curious, all but five of the usages are found in Torah and Former Prophets.[17] These instances cluster in a fairly restricted narrative context. As we shall see, Deuteronomy (34:5) and 2 Kings (18:12) each assign the title to Moses. Judges (2:8) employs the term once regarding Joshua. All the other references are found in Joshua. Unless this is mere happenstance, the possibility that this usage is hermeneutic should be given serious consideration.[18]

Hexateuch see fn 1. It is immaterial to me whether the putative canonizers meant consciously to accent this particular emphasis in the Deuteronomistic History. The effect would remain regardless of conscious intention. A similar decision to truncate a unified narrative for the purposes of canonical shaping may be seen in respect to the New Testament. The longest narrative complex, Luke–Acts, was divided so that the Acts portion would no longer follow only Luke, to which it was literarily and conceptually related, but would henceforth follow the four-gospel tradition.

16. Zimmerli and Jeremias list only 21 occurrences. Since twice the term appears in a Psalm title (Psalms 18:1; 36:1), perhaps they did not consider this part of the "original text" of Tanak. They list other occurrences as follows: *'abdî* = 62; *'abday* = 17; *'abd⁽ᵉ⁾kâ* = 92; *'ᵃbadèkā* = 20; *'abdô* = 23; *'ᵃbādâyw* = 16. See *The Servant of God*, 13.

17. Psalm 18:1; 36:1 (David); Isa 42:19 (unnamed Isaianic servant); 2 Chron 1:3; 24:6 (Moses).

18. Note Riesener's summarizing statement: "Die Beobachtung, dass sich mehr als die Hälfte aller Stellen, an denen Moses überhaupt den Titel יהוה עבד erhält, in dtr. Texten findet . . . zeigt, dass die Verwendung des Titels für Mose mit dem dtr. Sprachgebrauch und Denken in engem Zusammenhand gestanden haben muss" ("Der Stamm עבד" 191). Riesener obviously assumes the viability of Noth's thesis. Be that as it may, the references

'ebed YHWH as Applied to Moses and Joshua

Indicative of its possibly strategic usage, the initial application of the phrase *'ebed YHWH* to Moses and Joshua respectively appears in the two men's obituary notices. Though these notices are not formally identical in every detail, they are sufficiently similar to warrant comment. Moses' obituary appears at the end of Deuteronomy (34:5–8):

> So Moses the servant of YHWH (*'ebed YHWH*) died there in the land of Moab, according to the word of YHWH, and he buried him in the valley in the land of Moab opposite Bethpeor; but no man knows the place of his burial to this day. Moses was a hundred and twenty years old when he died; his eye was not dim, nor his natural force diminished (RSV: "abated"). And the people of Israel wept for Moses in the plains of Moab thirty days; then the days of weeping and mourning for Moses concluded.

Joshua's obituary notice is in the last chapter of Joshua (24:29–30):

> After these things Joshua the son of Nun, the servant of YHWH (*'ebed YHWH*) died, being a hundred and ten years old. And they buried him in his own inheritance at Timnath-serah, which is in the hill country of Ephraim, north of the mountain of Gaash.

The notice of Joshua's death is repeated in Judges (Judg 2:8–9):

> And Joshua the son of Nun, the servant of YHWH (*'ebed YHWH*) died at the age of one hundred and ten years. And they buried him within the bounds of his inheritance in Timnath-heres, in the hill country of Ephraim, north of the mountain of Gaash.

Moses' notice immediately follows YHWH's last words to him when the deity showed him the land of promise, reiterated the oath about giving the ancestors the land, and reminded the great leader that "you shall not go over there" (Deut 34:1–4).[19] The notice of Joshua's death comes right after he had sent the people away subsequent to his urging them to pledge themselves to serve YHWH exclusively (Josh 24:28; see vv. 22–27). In

---

clearly cluster in Joshua. Moses is called *'ebed YHWH* in the following passages in Former Prophets (excepting the one reference in Deuteronomy): Deut 34:5; Josh 1:1, 13, 15; 8:31, 33; 11:12; 12:6, 6; 13:8; 14:7; 18:7; 22:2; 2 Kgs 18:12.

19. See the treatment of the theological significance of Moses' death, actually and metaphorically, throughout Deuteronomy in Olson, *Deuteronomy and the Death of Moses*.

Judges the notice likewise occurs after Joshua had sent the people away.[20]
Both times the people went straight to their allotted territory in the land
of promise.

Moses was in Moab when he died. According to the Masoretic
Text, "he," apparently YHWH, buried him in a valley in Moab, opposite
Bethpeor. Presumably, this explains why his burial site remains unknown
"to this day" (Deut 34:5–6).[21] As for Joshua, it is not clear where he was at
the moment of death, but his place of burial seems not to be a secret—he
was buried in his own inheritance at Timnath-serah, which is in Ephraim's
hill country, and north of Gaash (Josh 24:30; Judg 2:9). The men's ages
are given in both notices: Moses is one-hundred and twenty, Joshua is
one-hundred and ten (Deut 34:7; Josh 24:29; Judg 2:8). Besides any "fac-
tual" information being divulged, at the literary and metaphorical level
this notation likely is a subtle reminder that Joshua never quite attains
Moses' stature.[22] Famously, Moses does not die a "natural" death, but "at
YHWH's command" (*'al-pî YHWH*), something further explicated by the
reminder that at the time of death Moses' "eye was not dim, nor his natural
force reduced" (RSV: "abated"; Deut 34:5, 7). The same is not claimed for
Joshua. Israel had a formal mourning period for Moses (Deut 34:8), but
no reaction on Israel's part is mentioned in Joshua's case. Though there is
no mourning for Joshua, significantly his death notice is bracketed by one
narrative and one summarizing statement, which together call attention to
his success in inducing Israel's obedient service to YHWH (Josh 24:22–27,
31). The notice in Judges is not framed in this manner, but the fact that
Israel served YHWH all of Joshua's days and all of the days of the elders
who outlived Joshua precedes the obituary (Judg 2:7).[23]

20. In both Joshua and Judges, the same exact phrasing is used: Josh 24:28; Judg 2:6:
wayšallaḥ Yᵉhôšûaʿ 'et-hāʿām.

21. MT: *wayyiqbōr 'ōtô.* The LXX differs. There "they," with no obvious antecedent,
bury Moses (*ethapsan*). However, in spite of the fact that "they," presumably meaning un-
specified Israelites, buried him, his grave site remains unknown (*kai ouk oiden oudeis tēn
taphēn autou heōs tēs hēmeras tautēs*).

22. See Butler, *Joshua*, 282. Drucker cites a rabbinic tradition which holds that ten
years were deducted from Joshua's life because he was not alacritous enough in the conquest of the land (Bamidbar Rabbah 22:6). Yehoshua/ *The Book of Joshua*, 468.

23. This generation gives way to the one which did not know *YHWH* or what the deity
had done in its behalf (Judg 2:10). After this the well-known "cycle of disobedience" in
Judges commences (Judg 2:11–23).

Beyond the similarities and dissimilarities of the two obituary notices, however, what is most important to keep in mind is that neither
Moses nor Joshua are accorded the title *'ebed YHWH* while they are alive.
For all their accomplishments, for all their domination of two great narrative complexes, for all the superlatives used to describe their extraordinary
leadership in Israel and their unrivalled service to YHWH, in the "story
world" which they inhabited and in which they were so very prominent,
they were never privileged to "hear" this title applied to them. Indeed,
even the less formal language of "my servant" (*'abdî*) with YHWH as
the speaker is used only one time in reference to Moses in Torah (Num
12:7–8). But even in this case Moses was not present—Miriam and Aaron
had sought out YHWH privately to "speak against" Moses (Num 12:1–6).
Every other time YHWH refers to Moses as "my servant" it points to the
past, after he is dead (Josh 1:2, 7; 2 Kgs 21:8; see Mal 3:22). Joshua does
not fare even that well. His obituary notices are the sole instances where he
is presented as YHWH's servant in any linguistic configuration.

One may conclude from this that the title *'ebed YHWH* bestowed
on Moses and Joshua was not for their personal benefit, so to speak.
Additionally, Israelites over whom Moses and Joshua presided would not
have known their leaders by this title either. As noted, every single time the
phrase *'ebed YHWH* appears in Deuteronomy or Joshua—and once in the
2 Kings passage (18:12)—it refers consistently to the two deceased leaders.[24] This suggests that the purpose for bestowing the title *'ebed YHWH*
on Moses and Joshua was a textual device to prompt a particular way
of reading their stories. Otherwise, it remains extremely curious that the
title is withheld until their demise. If being an *'ebed YHWH* was merely
an ordinary way of affirming the service to *YHWH* which these two men
rendered, why would they not have been so designated after any single
mighty deed which they performed in God's behalf and at God's command? Any one of their efforts, and most certainly any combination of
them, would surely have been enough to "earn" them the title. Why would
Moses have needed anything more than the exodus? Why would not the
fact that Joshua "fit the battle of Jericho" (Joshua 6) have been sufficient;
or, at the very least, why would he not have been accorded the title after
having taken the whole land "according to all that YHWH had spoken to

24. See fn 13 for the list of references.

Moses" (Josh 11:23)?[25] Yet, none of these spectacular feats qualify, so to say, Moses or Joshua to receive this accolade. It remains curious that both these outstanding advocates of YHWH would receive such a rare appellation in dual and strikingly similar death notices. Perhaps if only one of them had been called *'ebed YHWH* on the occasion of his death then the probability of an incidental reference could be conceded. But that is not the situation.[26]

There is a datum in the case of Joshua which lends some credence to the contention that granting him the title *'ebed YHWH* was not incidental. This has to do with Joshua's receiving a "promotion," as it were. At the beginning of the Book of Joshua the titles then held by the recently deceased Moses and his newly appointed successor Joshua are found side by side (Josh 1:1).[27] It needs to be kept in mind that once Moses is called *'ebed YHWH* in his obituary notice (Deut 34:5), the phrase is subsequently applied to him with little discernible pattern.[28] Yet, when the Book of Joshua begins, Moses' death is stressed—it is mentioned twice in the first two verses, once by the narrator and once by YHWH (Josh 1:1–2)—and his new title, first provided in the obituary notice, is repeated. Also, precisely because of Moses' recent demise, Joshua is now in the process of assuming command over Israel, having been commissioned just prior to his predecessor's final departure (Deut 31:7–8, 23). At the same time, though he is taking over for someone the narrative now calls *'ebed YHWH* and whom YHWH additionally calls "my servant" (*'abdî*) in Josh 1:1, Joshua

25. In spite of this and other summary statements that emphasize the total conquest of the land (see Josh 21:43–45), there are numerous texts indicating that much land remains to be conquered (e.g. Josh 13:1–7; 23:12–13). This is a major theme in Judges (Judg 1:27—2:5).

26. The fact that the LXX does not have a pattern anywhere close to the MT suggests that the latter has been edited in a particular direction, even if in a few cases the LXX was following a *Vorlage* different from the MT. The LXX uses varied terminology as well: Deut 34:5 (*oiketēs kyriou*); Josh 1:1 (no epithet); 1:3 (*ho pais kyriou*); 1:15 (no epithet); 8:31 (*ho therapōn kyriou*), 33 (*ho therapōn kyriou*); 11:12 (*ho pais kyriou*); 12:6 (*ho pais kyriou* [only once—twice in MT]); 13:8 (*ho pais kyriou*); 14:7 (*ho pais kyriou*); 18:7 (*ho pais kyriou*); 22:2 (*ho pais kyriou*); 22:4 (no epithet), 5 (*ho pais kyriou*); 2 Kgs 18:12 (*ho doulos kyriou*). See also 2 Chron 1:3 (*ho pais kyriou*); 24:16 (*anthrōpou tou theou*).

27. In the LXX, Moses is not referred to as δοῦλος κυρίου in Josh 1:1. Greenspoon cites Orlinsky as arguing that this means that the Hebrew *Vorlage* followed by the LXX in this instance simply did not have the phrase. See Greenspoon, "Theodotion, Aquila, Symmachus, and the Old Greek of Joshua," 82. See also Butler, *Joshua*, 3.

28. See fn 13. Butler asserts that applying the title of "servant" to Moses was "beloved by Deuteronomistic circles." *Joshua*, 8.

conspicuously retains his old title: Moses' "minister" (*mᵉšārēt Mōšeh*). But Joshua has just been advanced to a new level of leadership—he is taking over for Moses, with all the rights, privileges, and responsibilities that would naturally accrue to such a consequential position. Why does not his new "job" come with a new title? Would this not have been the natural place to affirm Joshua by granting him the same title as his vaunted predecessor? One "servant of YHWH" is taking over for another "servant of YHWH." Such a reasonable presumption notwithstanding, Joshua will not receive that title until his own obituary notice at the end of the book, as it was with Moses.

To be sure, it is no dishonor to be Moses' "minister." That is a lofty designation indeed, particularly in light of the way Moses looms as a protagonist in Torah. How should anyone conceive of the title of "minister" of Moses as somehow deficient? Nonetheless, being Moses' "minister" is not finally the same as being *'ebed YHWH*, however lofty a title it is in and of itself.

It is perhaps even more intriguing that the narrative withholds the more exceptional title from Joshua when such a concentrated effort is put forth to present him as Moses' virtual alter ego.[29] The plain fact is that for all Joshua's Moses-like qualities and experiences, it will be some time before he, like his predecessor, will attain the status of *'ebed YHWH*. And, as with Moses, that will happen only in his death notice.[30] Joshua may have taken over Israel as a "second Moses" at the outset of the story narrated in the Book of Joshua, but he will have to play this role still as Moses' "minister" and not as *'ebed YHWH*. In point of fact, as with Moses, Joshua will never learn that he has been so designated.

But should we have anticipated anything else? On any accounting Moses was the central figure for a longer time and in many more spectacular divine acts than Joshua was. If the one who encountered YHWH at the bush, announced God's delivery of Israel from the house of bondage, led the people forty years in the desert, presided over the enacting of the covenant, and became Israel's supreme prophetic representative and mediator between YHWH and the people (see Exodus 32–34), never attained the title of *'ebed YHWH* until after his death, why would we ever expect Joshua to have done so? Would it not have represented a diminution of Moses'

29. See Barth, "Moses, Knecht Gottes," 79.

30. Moore suggests that, at least in the Judges passage, *'ebed YHWH* was applied to Joshua by an editor. See *Judges*, 66.

own reputation to assign the *'ebed YHWH* title to Joshua when he took charge of Israel when his mentor never received the title in his lifetime? The question is all but rhetorical.

This brings us back to the different set of questions already hinted at above. Since only Moses and Joshua in all of Torah and Joshua (and the single reference in 2 Kings) are referred to with this special title, since the title for both men is first made known in their obituary notices, since there is no obvious reason why according this title should have been "delayed" if it were merely a way of affirming their generic service to YHWH, and since it seems that conferring the title has little to do with their several accomplishments or how the men should be compared to each other, then the question to be asked is: Why are they given the title at all?

I submit that the answer to that question lies not in considering Moses' and Joshua's numerous exploits and their ordinary service to YHWH. Rather, one very specific accomplishment that was achieved by both men deserves special attention. This accomplishment not only did not have to do with any of their more astonishing deeds, but had to do with an activity that was, ironically, "all talk and no action." To wit, attaching the title of *'ebed YHWH* to Moses and Joshua evokes their marked roles as spokespersons for YHWH. But even that assertion has to be more narrowly delimited. Obviously, both Moses and Joshua did a great deal of speaking during their respective ministries, and more specifically speaking in behalf of *YHWH*. For example, at the burning bush episode YHWH declares unreservedly to Moses, "I will be with your mouth and teach you what you shall say" (Exod 4:12). Similarly, after YHWH's initial speech to Joshua, the first thing the new leader does is "command" Israel (Josh 1:2–9, 10; *way(y)ᵉṣaw*). Both men clearly had multiple occasions to speak for their God. This was one of their main tasks. But there was one form of this crucial task that takes precedence over and is to be differentiated from everything else they ever uttered in God's stead, namely, their valedictory speeches. When Moses and Joshua speak for the final time in Israel's presence—Deuteronomy in Moses' case, Josh 23—24:15 in Joshua's—they engage in the very activity which is affirmed by the conferral of the title *'ebed YHWH*.

Moses' Valediction

The introduction to Deuteronomy sets forth how we are to regard what it is that Moses is about to say. The pending addresses are "the words" that Moses spoke to "all Israel" when they were "beyond the Jordan in the wilderness" at the eleventh month of the fortieth year of their epochal journey (Deut 1:1–2). There is no mistaking that the forthcoming speeches ultimately issue from YHWH: "Moses spoke . . . according to all that YHWH had given him in commandment . . . " (Deut 1:3). Just as important, what Moses is about to say to Israel takes place *after* the defeat of Sihon and Og (Deut 1:4). Actions of that sort are now over for Moses. What he is about to do in Deuteronomy is a completely different endeavor.

This endeavor requires Moses to "explain" or "interpret" (*bē'ēr*) the Torah (Deut 1:5). For the whole of Deuteronomy, this is what he does. In this regard, Olson points out that there are at least seventeen synonyms for "teaching" or its equivalent in the text of Deuteronomy.[31] This speaks to Moses' pedagogical and catechetical purpose. When Moses "speaks" Deuteronomy he is in the process of simultaneously interpreting the tradition and making sure that it will be passed on to each successive generation of Israelites. Not only does Moses affirm that "this is the commandment, the statutes and the ordinances" which YHWH commanded him to teach (Deut 6:1), but that these very same "words" Israel is to teach its children (Deut 6:6–9). Moses goes on to offer educational instruction in anticipation of the inevitable child's question: "When your son asks you in time to come, 'What is the meaning of the testimonies and the statutes and the ordinances which the Lord our God has commanded you?' then you shall say . . ." (Deut 6:20–21). The response that follows, which features recounting the exodus and giving of the land, concludes by reiterating the importance of being "careful to do" what has been commanded (Deut 6:21–25). In a subsequent passage where Moses drives home a similar point, he reminds Israel to pay special attention since he is now talking of children whom, because they have not "known" or "seen" God's "charge . . . statutes . . . ordinances . . . and commandments," the people themselves will one day be obligated to teach (Deut 11:1–2; 18–20). Still later Moses (with the elders) orders Israel to write "this Torah" on plastered stones upon their crossing of the Jordan (Deut 27:1–2, 8). Maintaining this em-

31. See Olson, *Deuteronomy and the Death of Moses*, 11. In addition to Deut 1:5, see for example 4:1, 5, 9,10, 14; 5:1, 31; 6:1, 7; 8:3; 11:19; 17:11; 20:18; 24:8; 31:19, 22; 33:10.

phasis on writing for the benefit of present and future Israelite generations, as Moses approaches his conclusion, he himself writes down the Torah and gives it to the priests and the elders (Deut 31:9). Then he commands that the Torah be read regularly (Deut 31:10–11). All are to be assembled, most especially the children "who have not known it" (Deut 31:12–13). There is even provision made for writing down the words of "this song" (see Deut 31:30—32:44), which was to serve as a witness to the people for what God had done in their behalf (Deut 31:19, 22). The Torah and the Song were to be preserved as a constant reminder to Israel of why God had elected them and what mission God had in mind for them, not to mention how serious were the consequences of forgetting this (Deut 31:24–29).[32]

Moses' words in Deuteronomy are a constant reminder of Torah and its indispensable role in the life of God's people. Olson argues that the claim is warranted that Deuteronomy even has the effect of "Torah-izing" the Pentateuch, for it is the only book in that complex that refers to itself as Torah or "this book of Torah."[33] As well, what Moses says in Deuteronomy should not be thought of as "law" in the sense of statutes for civil or political order. These are sermonic and theological interpretations which have an on-going pedagogical function for the people who now "hear" them as part of a written tradition. Poignantly, though Moses was unable to go with Israel into the land and continue in his role as a purveyor and interpreter of YHWH's word, by rendering what he said into written form his words would remain effective as long as the people possessed Torah.[34] The later designation of Scripture as "Moses and the Prophets" should be seen as something more than a conventional way to refer to the later community's canonical traditions. Most importantly, it should not escape our attention that precisely after Moses engages in this long work of interpretation, pedagogy, and catechesis he is, upon his death, for the very first time, given the title *'ebed YHWH*.[35]

---

32. Even the potential future king will have as his primary duty the writing down a copy of Torah. See Deut 17:18–20.

33. Olson, *Deuteronomy and the Death of Moses*, 8.

34. See Childs' remarks on the matter of Moses' "authorship" of Torah as well as its importance as a written document. *Introduction*, 132–35.

35. See Barth, "Mose, Knecht Gottes," 72. Note the remark by Krämer, "Das fünfte Buch Moses oder Deuteronomium ist nicht ein Gesetzbuch im juristischen Sinne des Wortes, sondern eine Sammlung von Predigten über die Gesetze." *Numeri und Deuteronomium*, 231. Riesener emphasizes the connection between Moses' servanthood and his proclamation of *YHWH*'s word. See "Der Stamm עבד," 190.

Joshua's Valediction

Biblical scholarship has tended to focus on the Book of Joshua either to ascertain the ostensible events that stand behind its accounts or to wrestle with the moral and theological problems presented by the "holy war" ideology it allegedly reflects.[36] For that reason, relatively less attention has been paid to Joshua's role as a "second Moses" precisely in respect to his being a preacher and a pedagogue. But Joshua, too, participates in a story that ends with his Deuteronomy-like valediction, even though by comparison it is a much shorter version than Moses'. Joshua's valediction is presented in two chapters (Josh 23:1–16; 24:1–15). The first occurs when Joshua summoned the whole community (no venue is given; Josh 23:1–2). The second takes place at Shechem in a covenant making ceremony.

However, in spite of the fact that Joshua's valediction should be read as such, this is hardly the first time he has functioned in this manner. Throughout the Book of Joshua considerable emphasis is placed on Joshua as one who commands, teaches, and preaches. When YHWH speaks initially to Joshua, reminding him of Moses' death, commanding him and the people to go over the Jordan into the land being given to them, promising them total success, outlining the boundaries, and pledging the divine presence at every turn (Josh 1:2–6), the deity goes on to caution Joshua to be careful to act according to all which Moses commanded in Torah (Josh 1:7). Further, this Torah is now a "book" (*sēfer*) that "shall not depart out of your mouth, but you shall recite (RSV: "meditate on") it day and night, that you may be careful to do according to all that is written in it" (Josh 1:8). For all the discussion about the Book of Joshua's reflection of militarism of one sort or another, *YHWH* says at this point not a word about any kind of military strategy, or troop levels, or preparations for armed conflict. All the deity's emphasis is on the divine promises and (Moses') Torah. Joshua is to be informed by Torah without wavering. But this is not a matter of private piety, for Joshua's duty is to keep always before

36. See Gerhard von Rad, *Der heilige Krieg im alten Israel*; R. Smend, *Jahwekrieg und Stämmebund*; F. Stoltz, *Jahwes und Israels Kirege: Kriegstheorien und Kriegserfahrungen im Glauben des alten Israel*; G. H. Jones, "Holy War or YHWH War," 642–58; M. Weippert, "'Heiliger Krieg' im Israel und Assyrien: Kritische Anmerkungen zu Gerhard von Rads Konzept des 'Heiligen Krieges im Alten Israel'," 460–93; P. Weimar, "Die Jahwekriegserzählungen in Exodus 14, Josua 10, Richter 4 und 1 Samuel 7," 38–73. For a summary of the theories of the conquest of the land see N. Gottwald, *The Tribes of Yahweh*, 191–219.

the people YHWH's words, Moses' words, and Torah itself. He is, it is important to remember, a "second Moses."

As the narrative unfolds, Joshua's ability to speak in a religiously authoritative manner is established in a variety of ways. He is depicted throughout as the receptor of divine commands,[37] as a substitute for, or as one who is in the guise of, Moses,[38] as the one who commands Israel in a variety of circumstances,[39] and as one who constantly affirms the authority of YHWH, Moses, and Torah.[40] Indeed, throughout Joshua four "voices" of authority merge as one. YHWH, Moses, Torah, and Joshua, in effect, all "speak" in unison. Perhaps nowhere is this more evident than in the "reading ceremony" in Joshua 8. This episode takes place right after the defeat of Ai (Josh 8:1–29). In response, Joshua builds an altar in Mount Ebal to YHWH (Josh 8:30). This was done explicitly according to Moses' command (note that Moses is referred to as *'ebed YHWH* in this instance) as written in Moses' Torah: "an altar of unhewn stones, upon which no man has lifted an iron tool" (Josh 8:31; see Deut 27:1–7, especially vv. 4–7). Likewise, in compliance with Torah, offerings were made to YHWH and a copy of the Torah was written upon the stones (Deut 27:8). At that point "all Israel"—including sojourner, native, elders, officials, judges— stand on opposite sides of the ark before the Levitical priests who carry it, half in front of Mount Gerizim and half in front of Mount Ebal, just as Moses—again referred to as *'ebed YHWH*—had commanded (Josh 8:33; see Deut 27:11–12). Then Joshua reads (*qārā'*) "all the words of the Torah, the blessing and the curse, according to all that is written in the Torah- book" (Josh 8:34). As though to insure that we do not miss the signifi- cance of what was taking place, the episode ends with repetitive emphasis: "There was not a word of all that Moses commanded which Joshua did not read before all the assembly of Israel, and the women, and the little ones, and the sojourners who lived among them" (Josh 8:35).[41] Clearly, in the

37. Josh 1:1–9; 3:8; 4:1–3, 8–9, 15–16; 5:2, 8–9; 6:2–7; 7:10, 13–15; 8:1–2, 18, 27; 10:8; 11:6, 15; 13:6; 15:13; 20:1–6.

38. Josh 1:5, 17; 3:7; 4:14; 5:13–15; 6:27; 9:24; 11:15.

39. Josh 1:10–11, 12; 2:1; 3:5–6, 9, 12–13; 4:4–7, 17, 21–22; 6:8, 10, 16–19, 22; 7:2, 19, 22; 8:4–8; 10:12–13, 14, 18–19, 22, 24–25, 27; 17:15; 18:3–7, 8; 22:8; 24:23.

40. Josh 1:13ff; 3:10; 4:23–24; 8:7, 32–35; 10:25 (using the same phrasing as *YHWH*); 22:1–5; 23:6–8, 11, 14–16; 24:14–15, 19–20, 25–27. Effectively, in the Book of Joshua there are four sources of authority, all of which are integrally related: *YHWH*, Torah, Moses, and Joshua.

41. There is a similar reference to "reading" (*qārā'*) Torah in 2 Kings. At first, upon

book which bears his name, Joshua cannot be relegated to a "political" or "military" leader; rather, he is someone who keeps Torah before the people in one setting after another, including this more formal public reading which is at the same time a reading of Torah and a fulfillment of it. In this instance, the "second Moses" is all but indistinguishable from the "first Moses," who pointedly is called *'ebed YHWH* twice in this reading scene.

Apart from the numerous instances in Joshua where Joshua speaks *for* YHWH or *as* Moses, or when he appeals to Torah explicitly or implicitly, his most developed and systematic engagement in pedagogical and catechetical activity is found in his two-chapter valediction at the end of the book. As noted, this is Joshua's own personal "Deuteronomy." In this setting he is as Moses-like as he ever gets.

The first part of Joshua's valediction (Josh 23:1–16) is clearly separated from all previous events: "A long time afterward, when YHWH had given rest to Israel from all their enemies round about, and Joshua was old and well advanced in years . . . " (Josh 23:1). That is, the "action" part of the Joshua narrative has been completed, as had been the case with Moses. For this address, Joshua summons the entire community: " . . . all Israel, their elders and heads, their judges and officers . . . " (Josh 23:2). What Joshua is about to say will be heard by the community as a whole, again, just as Moses began by speaking to "all Israel" (Deut 1:1). After acknowledging his advanced age, Joshua reminds his audience that they have seen all that YHWH did to the nations who had lived in the promised land (Josh 23:3). He goes on to reassure the people that he has already allotted to them not only the land already conquered but the land that remains unconquered (Josh 23:4). This presents no difficulty, for YHWH will persist in driving out these entrenched peoples until Israel is able to possess all the territory, a possession that is rooted in God's age-old promise (Josh 23:5).

Joshua then moves from assertion to admonition when he urges the people to be "very steadfast" to live according to everything written in Moses' Torah, making sure not to depart from its teaching even slightly (Josh 23:6). Here Joshua uses language reminiscent of YHWH when the deity first spoke to him (Josh 1:7). Joshua's appeal is completely based on religious concerns. Unless the people follow Torah unstintingly, they will

---

finding the "book" of Torah/the Covenant it is read more or less privately or with only a few hearers (2 Kgs 22:8, 10, 16). Afterwards, there is a public reading to the whole assembly in the pattern of Joshua 8 (2 Kgs 23:2). See as well the public reading of Torah in Nehemiah (8:3, 8, 18; 9:3).

be unable to guard against becoming mixed with the remaining peoples of the land. This is not about ethno-centrism or "tribalism"; rather, it has to do with Israel's religious purity and exclusive devotion to YHWH. That's why Israel must not so much as "remember" the names of the peoples' gods, let alone swear by them, or serve them, or bow down to them (Josh 23:7). Instead, Torah observance will enable the people to effect the command to "cleave" to YHWH as they have been doing all along (Josh 23:8). To be sure, calling Israel to stringent obedience is based completely on YHWH's prior gracious acts, which Joshua underscores by yet another reminder that everything achieved in taking over the land was the deity's doing—Israel's prowess was not a factor (Josh 23:9–10). Nonetheless, YHWH's working graciously in Israel's behalf does not preclude the necessity of their positive response. Should the people end up becoming in effect Canaanites by intermarrying and thus joining the remnant of the nations still unconquered, which will lead to the idolatry warned against (Josh 23:7), then an unthinkable punishment will be Israel's lot, namely, YHWH will discontinue driving out the inhabitants, making them instead a "snare," "trap," "scourge" and "thorn" in the eye. Even worse, the people will actually perish from the "good land" which their deity promised and gave to them (Josh 23:11–13).[42] This parallels Joshua's earlier reading "the blessing and curse" (Josh 8:34), which in turn alludes to similar material in Deut 27—28.

Joshua concludes this first "chapter" of his mini-Deuteronomy by calling to the people's attention once more that YHWH has kept every promise, but that it would be presumptuous on the people's part to treat this as a license to ignore the covenant that lies at the very heart of Torah. As Joshua makes abundantly clear, Torah rehearses tirelessly the wondrous, gracious acts of YHWH in Israel's behalf, for its benefit, and for the benefit of the eventual blessing of all the families of the earth (see Gen 12:1–3), while simultaneously reminding the people that adherence to Torah, reciting its story and following its precepts, must never be taken for granted (Josh 23:14–16). In this first half of his valediction, Joshua imitates Moses to a tee by proclaiming and interpreting YHWH's word.

---

42. For the possibility of Israel's disobedience leading it to become "Canaanite" and therefore suffering the consequences of that status, as well as the possibility for a Canaanite to become an Israelite with a Torah-like confession of faith, see Spina, *The Faith of the Outsider*, 52–71, especially 70–71.

The second time Joshua summons the entire Israelite community the location is explicit: Shechem (Josh 24:1).[43] This assembly, perhaps along with that in Joshua 8 (vv. 30–35), apparently fulfills Moses' command as given in Deut 27:4–5. The "reading" in Joshua 8, therefore, may be a literary doublet; nevertheless, in the final canonical shaping it serves as another gathering of all Israel so that Joshua could keep before the people the importance of Torah. If there is any added solemnity to this last effort of Joshua's to make the people keenly aware of YHWH's expectations, it is contained in the remark that they "presented themselves before God" (Josh 24:1).

Unlike the first installment of his valediction, where Joshua concentrated on YHWH's promise of the land and what the deity had in mind for the remaining inhabitants, this time Joshua goes all the way back to YHWH's initial call of the ancestors. More precisely, YHWH does this, for Joshua is at this point speaking in a prophetic mode: "Thus says YHWH, the God of Israel" (Josh 24:2). The oracle notes that prior to YHWH's involvement with Abraham, the ancestors "served other gods" (Josh 24:2). This is the first time Israel is told this.[44] Joshua continues—still speaking prophetically—by telling of God's taking Abraham from beyond the River, leading him to Canaan, making numerous his offspring, and giving him Isaac, then giving that patriarch Jacob and Esau. Though finally not part of the elect, God even had plans for Esau and his progeny, such that their possession was a function also of divine action (Josh 24:3–4).[45] The "history lesson" continues with the recollection that YHWH sent Jacob and his family into Egypt, then sent Moses and Aaron, whereupon the deity plagued Egypt and then rescued Israel from their bondage. The miraculous crossing of the water gets a little more attention, but the wilderness wanderings are summarized with the cryptic line that "you lived in the wilderness a long time" (Josh 24:5–7). As the oracle draws to a close, victories over the Amorites, deliverance from Balak the king of Moab,

43. The people were "summoned" (*qārā'*) in 23:1 as well.

44. The serving of other gods by the ancestors is at least hinted at in the story where Laban possessed *t'rāpîm*—usually regarded as "household" idols or gods—which Rachel stole just before the escape which Jacob engineered (Gen 31:19). Also, when Jacob later leads his family in a kind of religious reform, he starts by demanding that they "put away the foreign gods." Here different terminology is employed: *'elōhê hannēkār* (Gen 35:2).

45. See Spina's "Esau: The Face of God," in *The Faith of the Outsider*, 14–34. See, too, "The 'Face of God': Esau in Canonical Context," in *The Quest for Context and Meaning*, 3–25.

and the defeat of the men of Jericho as well as the "seven nations" are attributed to divine power (Josh 24:8–11). These are all gracious divine actions for Israel's sake and the basis for the relationship between YHWH and the elect people.

On the strength of all these actions performed by YHWH for Israel, Joshua in his prophetic mode finishes by calling on the people to decide uncompromisingly to "fear" and "serve" their deity. Regardless of their decision, whether for YHWH, or past (the gods of the ancestors) or present (the gods of the people in whose land they now dwell) deities, Joshua and his house opt without reservation for YHWH (Josh 24:14–15). Joshua has put before the people in his valediction what amounts to their only appropriate choice. What other response to grace of this magnitude makes any sense?

We pointed out above the accent on "serving" YHWH in this exchange between Joshua and the people, including at first their presumably blithe willingness to heed his invitation only to be stopped dead in their tracks until they perceive accurately what is being asked of them. Serving a "jealous" God meant that YHWH could not be served along with other deities. There was no way to negotiate a less demanding offer than Israel's having to "put away" any and all rivals. When Israel finally accepts the conditions of their commitment, Joshua makes a covenant with them—including statutes and ordinances—and writes "these words" in God's Torah-book. The occasion is marked by the placement of a "great stone" under an oak in YHWH's sanctuary (Josh 24:19–26). The last thing Joshua does is caution the people that this stone is a "witness" in that it has "heard" all the words which YHWH has spoken (through Joshua). Any false dealings on the part of the people would trigger the ability of the stone to witness to their faithlessness. With that, Joshua dismisses the people (Josh 24:26–28).

After having completed his valediction, Joshua dies. But when he dies he is instantly transformed from Moses' minister to *'ebed YHWH* (Josh 24:29). Poignantly and suggestively, like Moses, Joshua's death was immediately preceded by his final sermons to the people he had been commissioned to shepherd (see Num 27:18–22). And also like Moses, Joshua now has the same title. For both Moses and Joshua, their greatest accomplishments turn out not to be any of the astonishing divine deeds with which they are so grandly associated in the tradition. Joshua says as much when he insists that all the "mighty acts" are solely YHWH's doing, for " . . . I (i.e. YHWH) sent the hornet before you . . . it was not by your sword or by your bow. I gave you a land on which you had not labored, and cities which you had not built, and you dwell therein; you eat the fruit of vineyards and olive yards which you did not plant" (Josh 24:12–13). YHWH is the subject of all the strategic verbs in both Torah and the Book of Joshua. That is why for Moses and Joshua the stamp of approval for their prime vocational work involved their efforts at proclaiming, explaining, presenting, and implementing Torah for God's people, and what the people's response to that word should unquestionably be. That "ministry of the word" is in the end why we as readers of Scripture are to regard each of them as *'ebed YHWH*/"the servant of YHWH."

Conclusion

If in fact the *'ebed YHWH* nomenclature has been strategically applied to Moses and Joshua to bring into sharper focus their roles as preachers and interpreters of Torah, this surely has hermeneutic implications. The events recounted in Torah and Joshua (and the rest of the Former Prophets) are central and foundational to Israel's existence, identity, and mission as YHWH's people. None of the events are incidental. YHWH providentially orchestrates Israel's history either as a constitutive act, so that they would become the people the deity envisioned—a "kingdom of priests and a holy nation" (Exod 19:5–6)—or as an act of judgment, so that the process of Israel's sanctification would proceed apace (e.g., Exod 32–34). For this reason, these events and their religious and theological significance have to be remembered, recited, sung, celebrated, prayed, and rendered into ceremony and liturgy. In short, Israel's "past" has to become part of the warp and woof of Israel's divinely prompted self-reflection so that their "present" is always thoroughly infused with their keen awareness of who they are as God's people and what God wants to accomplish through them. This is why "these words"—"words" which are ultimately inclusive of Israel's comprehensive tradition—are to be "upon your heart," taught to the children, spoken of wherever one happens to be, bound as a sign on the hand, situated as frontlets between the eyes, and written on the doorposts of houses and gates (Deut 6:6–9).

What Moses and Joshua accomplish with their respective valedictory addresses to God's people is geared to this very matter. Their preaching, teaching, and interpreting is dedicated to the goal of insuring that Torah in all its dimensions becomes and remains integral to every aspect of Israel's life and work. For this reason, they not only *speak* and *interpret* Torah, they *write* down what they have spoken and interpreted. As a written entity, Torah can now be *read* as well. Because of this, the deaths of Moses and Joshua will prove inconsequential to the on-going efficacy of their ministry of the word. In effect, God's community will have Moses and Joshua with them as long as they have Torah. These men could have rendered no greater *service* to YHWH or YHWH's people.

The use of the *'ebed YHWH* terminology to highlight Moses' and Joshua's dual ministries of the word goes hand in hand with the way the Old Testament material has been shaped finally *as Scripture*. Regardless of the fact that historical Israel did not have a theologically robust conception of Scripture *per se*, as Judaism developed over the centuries, it edited and arranged its received traditions to function precisely as Scripture. This explains the inordinate emphasis on Torah as a *written* tradition, one that is to be regularly *read*.[46] I mentioned above Moses' provision in Deuteronomy 31 for reading Torah to the community so that they could receive the appropriate religious instruction in perpetuity, but the passage deserves to be quoted in full:

> At the end of every seven years, at the set time of the year of release, at the feast of booths, when all Israel comes to appear before YHWH your God at the place which he will choose, you shall read this law before all Israel in their hearing. Assemble the people, men, women, and little ones, and the sojourner within your towns, that they may hear and learn to fear YHWH your God, as long as you live in the land which you are going over the Jordan to possess. (Deut 31:10–13)

This reflects the importance of gathering the whole community for reading Torah. But such a ceremonial reading does not take away from other of Moses' admonitions to have Torah in mind virtually every minute

---

46. See the following references in Torah and Former Prophets to the Torah as written: Exod 24:3–4, 12; 31:18; 32:15–16, 19; 34:1, 27–28; Deut 4:13; 5:22; 6:9; 9:10; 10:2, 4; 11:20; 17:18; 27:3, 8; 28:58, 61; 29:19 [Eng v20], 20 [Eng v21], 26 [Eng v27]; 30:10; 31:9, 19 [refers to the song in chapter 32], 22 [refers to the song in chapter 32], 24; Josh 1:8; 8:31, 32, 34; 23:6; 24:26; 1 Kgs 2:3; 2 Kgs 14:6; 17:37; 22:13; 23:3, 21, 24. References to reading Torah are: Exod 24:7 [reading of the "book of the covenant"]; Deut 31:11; Josh 8:34–35; 2 Kgs 22:8, 10, 16; 23:2. For references to reading Torah outside of Torah and Former Prophets see: Neh 8:3, 8, 18; 9:3; 2 Chron 34:18, 24, 30.

of every day: " . . . you shall talk of them (i.e. "these words) when you sit in your house, and when you walk by the way, and when you lie down, and when you rise" (Deut 6: 7). YHWH, too, accents Moses' teaching when the deity reinforces to Joshua the importance of reciting (*hāgāh*) the Mosaic Torah "day and night" (Josh 1:7–8).[47]

Moses could not have left a greater legacy to Israel. For Israel to remain Israel and fulfill the mission that YHWH had all along planned, nothing was more crucial than keeping the Torah tradition alive. For all the efforts made by the prophets, throughout Former Prophets to remind Israel of their calling and their mission, the most extensive religious reform that is narrated is the one that came about through the reading of the written Torah. That Torah was, by all means, validated by a prophet(ess), but the reform itself was not instigated by one (2 Kgs 22:14–20). In that episode, a *book* (*sēfer*)—variously called *the book of Torah* or *the book of the Covenant* (e.g., 2 Kgs 22:8, 11; 23:2)—proved decisive.

Seeing how Moses became *'ebed YHWH* encourages the Church, which now reads the Moses story as part of its Scripture—now the Scripture of the Old and New Testament—not to lose sight of this most decisive part that he played. Proclamation and interpretation of Torah/Scripture was central to Moses' work and therefore central to the community he led. There are many ways that the Church appropriates its Scripture. Scripture is part of the Church's liturgy, its hymnology, its catechetical instruction, its art, its music, its doctrinal formulations, its theological reflection, its prayers, both corporate and private, its ethical deliberations, its evangelism, and its preaching. In all these activities the Church continues effectively to "recite day and night" and "interpret" Torah, which, as is well known, means "law" but so much more. Torah means "narrative," "story," "instruction," and even, as the good news about how God called a people to be the divinely appointed instrument for reconciling, redeeming, and restoring the whole created order, "Gospel." Indeed, the one whom Christians believe fulfilled Torah (Matt 5:17) and the prophets also engaged in the task of proclamation and interpretation (e.g., Luke 24:27), as did his apostles after him (e.g., Acts 8:26–39; 28:23). The Church which follows that apostolic lead is to enter into the same vocation in all the many ways that is possible.

---

47. The Jewish Publication Society translation has "recite," which is a much better rendering than "meditate," with its nuance of interior cogitation. A similar emphasis is found in Psalm 1 (v. 2).

Joshua should by no means take a proverbial "back seat" to Moses in terms of the proclamation and interpretation of Torah. In fact, Joshua's valediction serves in many ways to "rescue" the Book of Joshua from the rejection it has often faced in the Church. Because Joshua has often been seen from the perspective of ancient militarism or from anachronistically retrojected xenophobic ethnic attitudes, its usefulness to the Church has been all but lost. But Joshua makes clear in his valediction that the primary issue for Israel as God's people is its exclusive devotion to YHWH. The problem with the other "nations"—in historical terms none of whom likely existed when Joshua was composed—was their potential to compromise Israel with the lure of their gods. Israel was to be kept religiously pure, meaning its devotion to YHWH must not be jeopardized by syncretistic or idolatrous tendencies. Joshua is adamant that the choice for YHWH is not to be construed casually—commitment to this deity required all the allegiance the community could muster.

But this story where Joshua challenges Israel to realize how serious was the matter before them is not something that the Church now reads as though about a "past" event. As Scripture, Joshua's valediction keeps before the Church that at every moment and throughout the generations it must opt for the God who calls and sustains it. The Church is constantly confronted with the life and death decision of opting for the God without whom it would neither exist nor have a mission. Otherwise, it will inevitably and disastrously fall prey to the metaphorical equivalent of the deities whom the ancestors served or the gods of the people in those many lands where it now resides. When Joshua tells the people that regardless of their choice "[I] and my house, we will serve YHWH" (Josh 24:15), this recalls vocabulary found in the stories of Rahab and Achan earlier in the book. Rahab, a Canaanite prostitute, becomes part of Israel through her impressive confession of faith, perhaps the best confession of faith in the whole book (Josh 2:9–11). On that basis, she asks to be spared from the coming destruction of her city. Not only does she appeal for her whole "house" to be saved, the spies agree to her conditions regarding her whole family (Josh 2:13, 18). When the city is destroyed, Rahab and her house are spared and become part of Israel "to this day" (Josh 6:17, 25).

Conversely, the quintessential Israelite Achan—no one has a more impressive genealogy in the book (Josh 7:1)—breaks faith and brings potential judgment on the whole community (Josh 7:10–12). He is eventually discovered and made to pay the ultimate penalty. But he is not the only one under judgment. His entire family suffers with him (Josh 7:24). This story about Achan is in antipodal relationship to the story about Rahab. At the hermeneutic level, these two stories have the effect of keeping before Israel the possibility that anyone who confesses faith in the manner of Rahab may become part of Israel while any who egregiously violate faith risk removal from the community.[48] It is more than sobering to read this warning in the very context where Israel is given one of the best "reports" on its service to YHWH. Joshua warned an obedient Israel (Josh 24:31)! The Church must never relax its vigilance about opting consciously for God or be tempted to believe that the choice Joshua puts now to the people of every generation via their Scripture is an *easy* choice, or a matter of the culture into which one has been accidentally born, or a decision that may in the modern world be smugly dismissed in the name of *multiculturalism* or *diversity*. In short, when read *as Scripture*, Joshua cannot be ignored and set aside as so many conquest stories, "ethnic cleansing" accounts, land allotments, or primitive justification for occupying foreign land. Joshua in his role as *'ebed YHWH*, along with the eventual rendering of Joshua into *Scripture*, requires the community never let up its collective guard in "choosing" for the Lord while rejecting all that would compromise that choice.

Moses and Joshua are all but incomparable in light of the events in which they have by YHWH's inscrutable call played such vital parts. It is precisely the extraordinary nature of those events that makes so incredible that they would receive their loftiest affirmation with a title designed to accent their "ministry of the word." That ministry, now wondrously enscripturated and offered for the life of the Church, the Body of Christ, which believes it is in continuity with Israel, God through the Holy Spirit graciously sustains. These two *'abdê YHWH* speak to us still.

Bibliography

Barth, Christoph. "Mose, Knecht Gottes." In *Parrhesia: Karl Barth zum 08. Geburtstag*, 58–81. Zurich: EVZ, 1966.

Butler, Trent C. *Joshua*. Word Biblical Commentary, 7. Waco, TX: Word, 1983.

Childs, Brevard S. *Introduction to the Old Testament as Scripture*. Philadelphia: Fortress, 1979.

Davis, Ellen. "The Poetics of Generosity." Unpublished essay.

Drucker, Reuven. *Yehoshua/The Book of Joshua*. Brooklyn: Mesorah, 1982.

---

48. See Spina, *The Faith of the Outsider*, 52–71.

Gottwald, N. *The Tribes of Yahweh.* Maryknoll, NY: Orbis, 1979.

Greenspoon, Leonard. "Theodotion, Aquila, Symmachus, and the Old Greek of Joshua." *Eretz-Israel* 16 (1982) 82–91.

Jones, G. H. "Holy War or YHWH War." *VT* 25 (1975) 642–58.

Krämer, Karl Fr. *Numeri und Deuteronomium.* Die Heilige Schrift für das Leben erklärt II/1. Freiburg: Herder, 1955.

Lindhagen, Curt. *The Servant Motif in the Old Testament.* Uppsala: Lundequitska Bokhandeln, 1950.

Moore, George F. *Judges.* ICC. Edinburgh: T. & T. Clark, 1895.

Mowinckel, Sigmund. *He That Cometh.* Translated by G. W. Anderson. Oxford: Blackwell, 1959.

Noll, K. L. "Deuteronomistic History or Deuteronomic Debate? (A Thought Experiment)." *JSOT* 31 (2007) 311–45.

Noth, Martin. *Überlieferungsgeschichtliche Studien: die sammelnden und bearbeitenden Geschichtswerke im Alten Testament.* 2nd ed. Tübingen: Niemeyer, 1957. [Available as *The Deuteronomistic History.* Translated by J. Doull et al. JSOTSup 41. Sheffield: JSOT Press, 1981]

Olson, Dennis T. *Deuteronomy and the Death of Moses: A Theological Reading.* Overtures to Biblical Theology. Minneapolis: Fortress, 1994.

Rad, Gerhard von. *Der heilige Krieg im alten Israel.* Göttingen: Vandenhoeck & Ruprecht, 1962.

Riesener, Ingrid. *Der Stamm עבד im Alten Testament.* BZAW 149. Berlin: de Gruyter, 1979.

Ringgren, Helmer. "עבד, 'Abad." In *Theologisches Wörterbuch zum Alten Testament,* edited by G. Johannes Botterweck et al., 5:999–1003. Stuttgart: Kohlhammer, 1986.

Rutledge, Fleming. "What the Angel Said." In *The Bible and the New York Times,* 7–12. Grand Rapids: Eerdmans, 1998.

Sanders, James A. *Torah and Canon.* Philadelphia: Fortress, 1972.

Seitz, Christopher. "The Call of Moses and the 'Revelation' of the Divine Name: Source-Critical Logic and Its Legacy." In *Theological Exegesis: Essays in Honor of Brevard S. Childs.* Edited by Christopher Seitz and Kathryn Greene-McCreight, 145–61. Grand Rapids: Eerdmans, 1999.

Smend, Rudolf. *Jahwekrieg und Stämmebund.* FRLANT 84. Göttingen: Vandenhoeck & Ruprecht, 1963.

Spina, Frank Anthony. "The 'Face of God': Esau in Canonical Context." In *The Quest for Context and Meaning: Studies in Biblical Intertextuality in Honor of James A. Sanders,* edited by Craig A. Evans and Shemaryahu Talmon, 3–25. Biblical Interpretation Series 28. Leiden: Brill.

———. *The Faith of the Outsider: Exclusion and Inclusion in the Biblical Story.* Grand Rapids: Eerdmans, 2007.

Stoltz, Fritz. *Jahwes und Israels Kriege: Kriegstheorien und Kriegserfahrungen im Glauben des alten Israel.* Zürich: Zwingli, 1972.

Vogt, Peter T. *Deuteronomic Theology and the Significance of Torah: A Reappraisal.* Winona Lake, IN: Eisenbrauns, 2006.

Weimar, P. "Die Jahwekriegserzählungen in Exodus 14, Josua 10, Richter 4 und 1 Samuel 7." *Biblica* 57 (1976) 38–73.

Weippert, Manfred. "'Heiliger Krieg' im Israel und Krieges im alten Israel." *ZAW* 84 (1972) 460–93.

Zimmerli, Walther, and Joachim Jeremias, *The Servant of God.* Translated by Harlod Knight et al. Studies in Biblical Theology. Naperville, IL: Allenson, 1957.

7

Death Binds, Death Births*

Stanley D. Walters

As a boy, I used to run down the street to meet our mailman. I knew him well, Mr. A. E. Smith, for he attended our church and was the grandfather of one of my schoolmates. I used to try to wheedle our mail out of him before it was our turn—hoping there would be something for me. Sometimes I met him at the corner a block away, where the yard was edged with a brick wall, and I would walk along it with him. Encountering Mr. Smith there one morning, I jumped off the wall and landed beside him on the sidewalk. He looked at me, shifted his mail bag, and said, "That's all right for you, but I'm not as supple as I used to be." He pronounced it "soopel," as if it were an unusual word.

Now that I'm a grandfather myself, I know what he meant. I'm not as supple as I used to be, and I don't jump off walls very much any more. And I also know that some of that stiffness shows that death is nearer to me now than when I ran to meet the mailman. As death approaches, it slows us down, and its goal is to end movement altogether.

In Psalm 18, King David says, "The cords of death encompassed me." It's a telling metaphor, offering a clear and apt image of death's intention to restrict and to bind. The expression, "the cords of death" / "Sheol," occurs four times in the Old Testament, and this paper is first of all about these words and their theological force. Here are the four texts (ESV) in canonical order; the table (p. 91) gives them (plus a fifth to be discussed later in the paper) with English translations as well as their ancient renderings in Greek and Aramaic.

* This paper is dedicated to the memory of Brian Schaal, and in honor of his parents, Sue and Peter, and of Wendy, Bear, and Melody.

1. For the waves of death encompassed me,
    The torrents of destruction assailed me,
  The *cords of Sheol* entangled me;
    The snares of death confronted me. (2 Sam 22:5–6)
2. The *cords of death* encompassed me;
    The torrents of destruction assailed me. (Psalm 18:5)
3. The *cords of Sheol* encircled me;
    The snares of death confronted me. (Ps 18:6)
4. The *cords*[1] *of death* encompassed me;
    The pangs of Sheol laid hold on me;
    I suffered distress and anguish. (Ps 116:3)

	KJV > NRSV	JPS	LXX	Targum
2 Sam 22:6	cords	snares	ὠδῖνες "pangs" σχοινία "cords"	מַשִׁרִית (רֹשִׁיעִין) "armies of men"[a]
Ps 18:5	cords	ropes	ὠδῖνες Aquila: σχοινία Symm:[b] τρώσεις[c]	עָקָא "distress" with a plus referring to a woman in childbirth
Ps 18:6	cords	ropes	ὠδῖνες	מַשִׁרִית (חִיבִין) "armies[d] of (sinners)"
Ps 116:3	cords (RSV+: snares)	bonds	ὠδῖνες	מִיעָר (מָאוּת) "sickness of death"
Ps 119:61	cords (REB: crowds)	ropes	σχοινία	חֵעִים (רֹאִיעִישׁ) "band of (wicked men)"

[a] This is Targum Onkelos; Targum Jonathan adds the same long simile that is found for Ps 18:5; see note 15.

[b] These variants are found in Field, *Origenis Hexaplorum* (Hildesheim: Olms, 1964) 2:109.

[c] The uncommon noun means "a wounding," and is connected with the verb τρώω / τιτράσκω ("to wound, injure"), which, in childbirth, is the opposite of τίκτω ("give birth").

[d] So Edward Cook; see his translation at <www.tulane.edu/~ntcs/pss/tg_ps_index.htm>, accessed 10/11/07.

1. Here, strangely, the RSV, NRSV, and ESV translate "snares," which either interprets the cords as snares or tacitly emends the text. The KJV reads "sorrows," but the ERV and ASV correctly read "cords."

The Word(s)

The segholate noun *hevel* "cord, rope," *havlê-* "cords of . . ." occurs in the Bible fifty times.[2] In *concrete contexts* it can refer to tent cords (Isa 33:20, 23), a trap or snare (Ps 140:6; Job 18:10), a measuring line (2 Sam 8:2; Amos 7:17); it can have the extended meanings "portion of land" (Deut 3:3, 13, 14; Josh 17:14) and even a "band of prophets" (1 Sam 10:5, 10). The texts I just quoted, however, show the word in *metaphoric use* referring to death and what follows.

The language of the immediate context of these instances—torrents, snares, toils, torments—implies violence and perhaps suddenness. If death comes unexpectedly, it is a snare, sprung suddenly and fatally. The two verbs used, *'pp* and *sbb*, speak of encircling and surrounding, suggesting death as immobilizing. This is in fact the human experience of death: it binds. This is true whether it comes *suddenly*, striking down the young in the midst of exuberant sport and pleasure and the mature in the midst of business and family routine, or *gradually*, in the slow and natural processes of aging and senescence, of which Chief Inspector Morse speaks when he turns fifty and finds himself "on the cemetery side of the semi-centenary mark."[3]

Before it, we lose the power to move and act, until, when it is complete, there is utter stillness. Sometimes—as with the grandfathers I've mentioned—it winds itself slowly about us in Lilliputian threads, and we feel its restraining power only gradually; but it comes with cords to bind.

Cords, ropes, and even snares, then, evoke this perspective on death: a severe metaphor, to be sure, but appropriate, and realistic. The ropes of death—*funes mortis*—lead naturally to *rigor mortis*.

The earliest readers of the Bible, however, knew a way of softening the harshness of this figure. There is a pun to be had, for the Hebrew word "cords of" (*havlê*) looks and sounds like another word with another meaning. That word is *hevlê* "pangs of," meaning the pains that accom-

---

2. So Abraham Even-Shoshan, *A New Concordance of the Bible* (Jerusalem: Kiryat Sepher, 1983) 344. Among them are six instances of the construct plural in *patah*, a group that the masorah has specifically noted. It does so at Josh 17:5, "the ten *portions* of Manasseh," where the word *havlê* receives the observation that this form is unique, but all forms with prefixed *beth* are vocalized the same way. The only regular construct plurals of the noun *hevel* are those with prefixed *beth*, and one might think that the note draws attention to this group and to the spelling with *patah* as the correct form.

3. Morse is the elegant Oxford detective in Colin Dexter's novels, played memorably on television by the late John Thaw.

pany birth.[4] This second meaning is a way out of the bleak realism of the expression "*cords* of death": you use the other word, and speak of the "*pangs* of death."

The one is a plain-sense metaphor of death as that which binds, while the odd second expression points to the nursery side of the semi-centenary mark, to the other end of life from death, to the throes and contractions that lead to new life. With that one stroke, the picture on the screen changes. In Israel's faith, death is both the end of life and the beginning of a new and different existence; it is no longer a restriction, a binding, an end. Rather, it is a new beginning, and it births us into a world and an existence we have never known.[5]

This second meaning points to the idea of the resurrection of the dead (Dan 12:2; Isa 26:19), which it intimates in quiet and unobtrusive hope. The people of the covenant expect in death to be born into a new existence, all under the watchful care of the Creator. Saint Paul says that death is the last enemy to be destroyed, and as the Bible gives us this word-play, we see already the rhetorical destruction of death.

That's what the Bible does with the earthy realism of threatening bonds and final restraint: it transforms the image into the heavenly realism of God's larger plan. That's what the Bible does with death: it leads us to think of life in larger and different terms, and it is the reality of that life and its Lord that gives us our greatest comfort whenever we confront death.

It follows that this paper is actually about two words instead of one, about the near-homophones *hevel* and *hēvel* and their theological force in the word-play involving the plural construct forms *havlê* and *hevlê*, one spelled with an /a/-vowel (patah) and one with an /e/-vowel (seghol). The /a/-word means "cords of," the /e/-word means "pains of."

There are immediately questions to be addressed. How do double-meanings arise? and how do they work? What is the evidence for this one? How does the Hebrew of the Masoretic Text read? And how do double-meanings in other languages work in translation? Why do our English

---

4. The absolute form is *hevel*, and Even-Shoshan lists eight occurrences of this noun, all having to do with childbirth (Isa 13:8; 26:17; 66:7; Jer 13:21; 22:23; 49:24; Hos 13:13; Job 39:3).

5. As a rhetorical parallel, in an unrelated field, I note a review of Edward Short that mentions John Henry Newman's prolonged deliberation over his conversion to Roman Catholicism, especially a lengthy relinquishing of all that he would be leaving behind. However, Short says, Newman's "deathbed was also a cradle"; Edward Short, "Bound for Rome," *The Weekly Standard* (Nov. 6, 2006) 34.

translations give only the first meaning (see p. 91)? The paper now moves to address these matters.

How Double Meanings "Work"

I see this word-play arising at a time when the Hebrew text is being transmitted only in consonantal form; both words are identical on the page, being spelled with the same consonants, חבל‬. The droll beauty of unvocalized Hebrew text—as many beginning Hebrew students have discovered—is that double readings can more easily arise, and the reader slips easily into both of them. With our texts, I suppose the reading tradition came to cherish both readings for theological reasons. The second meaning does not arise out of the text, for the text has entirely to do with death and its gloomy aftermath. Rather, it comes into the reader's mind, triggered by the word-play, and it reverses the negative force of the text. The student who learns the reading tradition thus learns the possibility of the double meaning and its significance, and the congregation who hears the text expounded does so as well. Indeed, it almost requires a homily to spell it out, and that's probably how it came about to start with. The witty homilist says, "Don't say *ḥavlê*, say *ḥevlê*. Death *binds*, but it also *births*! To faith, death is not the terminator, but the begetter."[6]

A double reading is always a loose figure, based first of all on sound rather than meaning. In the present case, the first meaning ("Death binds") works, the second one ("Death births") is, on the surface, odd; it is allusive rather than obvious. Attempts to understand it literally will fail because the expression has been coined as a second meaning and requires the first one to make full sense. This is essential to the pun. Death is pregnant? has birth contractions?[7] Well, only in a manner of speaking. But the metaphor of pregnancy and birth would never have arisen in this context at all had not the existence of the homophone brought it to mind. The one single point is enough: to pass through death is not to come to an end, to subside

---

6. Puns cannot be translated, only re-invented. These two Hebrew words barely differ from each other. I cannot come up with anything in English as close as they, but here are a few tries that give a sense of paranomasia. "Death binds your girth, then brings your birth." "In death, your nemesis is your genesis." "Death's curb is also your crib" (see n. 5 above).

7. See Robert Bratcher, "'Having Loosed the Pangs of Death,'" *The Bible Translator* 10/1 (1959) 19 [18–20], who struggles with this difficulty and finally concludes that "pangs" really means "cords," thus really telescoping two different words into one.

into rigor mortis, but to find a beginning, to enter a new existence, to rise to vigor vitalis.

Nevertheless, for the second meaning to have its full force, the first meaning needs to be in mind.

Since these texts were first written without any vowels, how can there be any evidence for a double reading? I mention two.

First Evidence: The Masoretic Vocalization

The reading tradition for unvocalized text may be replete with double meanings, but when such text comes to be vocalized, a choice has to be made; the same is true of a translation. Both vocalization and translation will mean the end of double readings, unless ways can be found to preserve them both. How do you keep both meanings alive?

One way the Bible does so is by preserving the second meaning, the unusual and odd reading, in the written text. The savvy reader can recover the first reading, which is obvious enough, and then go on to grasp the second reading and thus explain the text. The Masoretic text preserves the odd reading to keep it from being lost altogether.

When the four texts we are discussing finally came to be vocalized, the masoretic scholars gave them the vowels of the second meaning—*ḥevlê* instead of *ḥavlê*. Their form is anomalous if they are supposed to mean "cords, ropes"; their form connects them instead with *ḥēvel*, "pangs." I've already argued that "cords of death" is a realistic metaphor for death; a metaphor "pangs of death" is unexpected. True, the approach of death may be painful and even prolonged, but its final arrival is the end, and the figure of birth seems inappropriate. In spite of the fact that the translation "cords" yields a very satisfactory sense,[8] the Masora marks these forms as a distinct group by vocalizing the consonants *ḥbly* with /e/ instead of /a/. This suggests the word-play, and is our first evidence for the double reading.

Thus, we owe the "binds/births" view of death and what follows to the masoretic vocalization of these four texts. I think it is a statement about death that deserves not to be lost, whatever the subsequent history of the reception of these texts.

Why our English translations do not render it that way is another question, that I take up later in the paper.

8. Indeed, some dictionaries and concordances—including Even-Shoshen—list these very passages under the word *ḥevel* "cord."

A parenthetical detail for specialists who might argue that we should not put too fine a point on the vocalization of segholate nouns, and that the noun *ḥevel* "cord" may simply have two forms of the plural construct.[9] I grant that two differing forms could easily arise. But the two nouns are distinguished in form within two separate books of the Bible: Hos 11:4, "I led them *beḥavlê 'ādām*, with *cords of* kindness," and Hos 13:13, *ḥevlê yôlēdâ* "The *pangs of* childbirth come for Ephraim"; and Job 36:8, "Caught *beḥavlê 'ônî* in the *cords of* affliction," and Job 39:3 of animals giving birth by expelling *ḥevlēhem* "their foetuses."[10] And instances of both forms seem to be grouped together by virtue of masoretic attention and activity: there are those with pataḥ in the group with prefixed beth (see n. 2 above), and those with seghol in the group speaking of death and Sheol. The gathering of the two forms each around a central feature is against utter randomness.

Second Evidence: The Septuagint

The second thing to say is that the Septuagint also confirms the word-play's existence at an early stage of the text's transmission. Throughout its translation of the Hebrew Bible, the Greek almost universally offers σχοινία "cords" as an equivalent to *ḥevel*. But in the four quoted places, ὠδῖνες appears instead, "the pangs of death/Sheol." The Greek ὠδίν otherwise stands in the LXX entirely opposite *ḥevel* "birth-pangs" and in contexts having to do with childbirth.

It has often been assumed that this was simply a mistake by the translator, who did not recognize the problem of words that may look and

---

9. The morphology and development of the segholate nouns has been carefully worked out by the grammarians, and the patterns are well-known. *Ḥevel* is derived from the primitive form *qatl*, and *ḥēvel* from the primitive form *qitl*. See Wilhelm Gesenius, *Gesenius' Hebrew Grammar*, 2nd English edition, trans. E. Kautzsch, ed. A. E. Cowley (Oxford: Clarendon, 1910) §84a-d, §93, but especially Paul Joüon, *Grammaire de l'Hebreu Biblique* (Rome: Institute Biblique Pontifical, 1947) §88Ca-b, h, §96Ae, who explains the /e/-vowel and speaks of the easy contamination between *qatl* and *qitl* forms. A number of primitive *qitl* forms have become *qatl* in Hebrew, both because some forms of both nouns are identical, and because some forms are "more sonorous" than others. "In the same noun one finds forms that suggest a *qatl* and forms that suggest a *qitl*; it is therefore often difficult or impossible to tell if a certain noun is originally a *qatl* or a *qitl*, or if the two forms existed simultaneously" (§96Af, p. 238).

10. Marvin H. Pope, *Job*, Anchor Bible (Garden City, NY: Doubleday, 1973) 306.

sound alike.[11] With all awareness of the fallibility of scribes, including myself, I still want to look beyond that assumption.

The LXX does what the masoretic vocalization has done: it puts the odd second reading in the text so that it will not be lost, and leaves the reader to know or figure out the standard reading. Since (as I think) both senses of the letters חבל י were known at the time of the LXX's translation, the Greek translation enables both readings—but now in a language where the aural pun no longer works, and so the explanatory homily is that much more important.[12]

But how long can both senses survive translation? Without them both, the rhetorical force of the second meaning is greatly weakened, and the sense becomes obscure. But I believe there is other evidence for the double reading, "the cords/pangs of death," and I now follow this paronomasia into its early appearances in the New Testament and in the Targum. This will show that, at least for a time, both senses remained alive, even when parts of the tradition did not accept the second reading.

The New Testament

When New Testament writers come to express their faith that Jesus has been raised from the dead, the theological double reading of this paper is at hand for them—in the LXX if not also in the Hebrew text. Paul speaks of Jesus as "the firstborn from the dead" (Col 1:18), as does Rev 1:5. "Firstborn," of course, is royal language in the Hebrew Bible (Psalms 2:7, 89:28), and not unexpected in a messianic context,[13] but the genitive τῶν νεκρῶν "from the dead" has specific reference to the Christian application—since the OT kingship texts do not refer to the king's death. I would understand the expression, "the firstborn from the dead," as also an allusion to the LXX's language in our texts, "the birth-pangs of death."

A second citation takes this further. In Acts 2:24, Jesus' disciple Peter claims, "God raised Jesus up, *loosing* the pangs of death, because it was not possible for him *to be held* by it." Here the reference to our texts amounts to quotation from the LXX, as the marginal cross-references of the Nestle-

---

11. See Bratcher, "'Having Loosed,'" 18.

12. To those who think that the LXX's reading might result from Christian editing to bring it into conformity with Acts 2:24 (see section on the NT below), I note that the masoretic vocalization would not have been influenced by Christian interpretation.

13. See also Rom 8:29; Heb 1:6; and Rev 2:8.

Aland text of the Greek NT assert. These words not only connect "the pangs of death" with a new existence that follows death, but the accompanying language *shows awareness of both meanings* of the Hebrew expression: of the second ("pangs"), of course, but also of the first, namely, "cords." The evidence for this is in the two verbs "be held" and "loosing," which language is appropriate to cords but not to pangs. (I grant that ὑπ' αὐτοῦ "by it" refers to death and not to the pangs/cords, but the power of death to bind is precisely the original meaning of the phrase.)

This quotation often been a difficulty for commentators on Acts because of the incongruity between the noun "pangs" and the verbs of holding and loosing. In their classic commentary, Foakes-Jackson and Lake speak of it as "a fixed phrase capable of new combinations with verbs of holding, loosing, etc."[14] I suggest rather, that, as the earliest Christians spoke of their faith in Jesus' resurrection, and as Luke collected material for the book of Acts, both senses of the Hebrew expression were still current, and the oddity was accepted for that reason.

The Targum

The Targum's handling of these passages also shows awareness of both homophones, but in ways that move interpretation away from the force of the double meaning. Please refer back to page 91.

Texts #1 and #3 know the original meaning "cords," but they take the word in its extended sense of a band or troop, exactly as Samuel uses it when he guides Saul to a *ḥevel nevi'îm* "a band of prophets" in 1 Samuel 10:5, 10. The *ḥevlê Šeʾôl*, then, are hellish *bands*, "*armies* of evil men/sinners." Thus Targum Onkelos avoids the double meaning altogether. This rendering presumes the /a/-vocalization (with pataḥ), and therefore either an unvocalized text or one different from the MT, but the plus in Targum Jonathan (see n. 15) implies the /e/-reading.

Where text #3 ignores (or refuses) the possible double reading of cords/pangs, #2 and #4 assume it—but give it a meaning that cannot be connected with resurrection. Text #2 uses the general word *'q* "trouble, distress," and, in an addition to the biblical passage,[15] speaks of a woman

14. F. J. Foakes Jackson and Kirsopp Lake, *The Beginnings of Christianity, Part I: The Acts of the Apostles, Vol. IV: English Translation and Commentary* (London: Macmillan, 1933) 23.

15. "Distress has surrounded me, like a woman who sits on the birthstool and has no strength to give birth and so is in danger of death . . ." So Edward Cook (see URL in n.

in labour who has no strength to give birth and is in danger of death. Similarly, Symmachus' noun τρώσεις seems to allude to miscarriage. The associations here with childbirth imply knowledge of the double-reading, but give interpretations that imply the very opposite of birth: *ḥevlê māwet* is not a metaphor at all, sometimes birth pangs actually kill. And in usage #4, the rendering "sicknesses of death" softens the meaning of *ḥevlê* from pangs to sicknesses—but it is fatal illness, again implying just the opposite of new life. These renderings accept and follow the Masoretic vocalization with seghol, and are therefore evidence for the double meaning.

That is, as the Targum takes shape, the influence of both nouns is alive in the renderings of three of our passages. But the Targum does not preserve the specific double meaning implicit in the OT paronomasia— namely intimating the resurrection of the dead—for none of the Targum's language is as specific as the MT's or the Septuagint's.

We might see in the Targum's wariness a certain hermeneutic auster-ity, as if to restrain an excessive figuration or to reduce theological infer-ences based on a mere paronomasia or to reject a far-fetched pun. But it's also possible that polemic interests have guided these choices. Once the expression "pangs of death" has been appropriated by the New Testament, the Targum might wish to provide interpretations of the Hebrew text that do not point to life after death—"Christians may find that in the Septuagint, but the Hebrew means something else!" This protects the text from the meaning that Christians give to it, but at the cost of its comfort in the face of death.

The Targum's divergent readings of our four texts, then, point to Jewish-Christian engagement over the meaning of the book of Psalms. As soon as Christians began to claim Psalm 116:3 for Jesus, rabbinic scholars would have been at work providing answers to those claims. In such a way (in very different times and places) Justin Martyr provided Trypho with texts and arguments, and Radaq provided readers of his commentary on the Psalms with rebuttals to texts used by Christians.[16]

5). The same in Daniel Harrington's translation of 2 Sam 22:6 in Targum Jonathan, "For distress surrounded me like a woman who sits upon the birth-stool, and she does not have strength to give birth, and she is in danger of dying. A company of sinners terrified me"; Daniel J. Harrington and Anthony J. Saldarini, *Targum Jonathan of the Former Prophets,* Aramaic Bible 10 (Wilmington, DE: Glazier, 1987) 200.

16. See, for example, his explanations of Psalm 2 in David Ḳimḥi, *The Longer Commentary of R. David Ḳimḥi on the First Book of Psalms,* trans. R. G. Finch (London: SPCK, 1919). See also David Berger, *The Jewish-Christian Debate in the High Middle Ages*

Through the Centuries

And now Ps 119:61, where the consonants *ḥbly*, meaning "cords," are vocalized *ḥevlê* instead of *ḥavlê*.

> Though the *cords of* the wicked ensnare me,
> I do not forget your law.

This verse was the big surprise to me as I worked on this paper. The vocalization with seghol clearly groups it with the four death/Sheol texts, but there is no way that "pangs" can serve as a second meaning here. I think that in the on-going interpretation of these four texts—and particularly if polemic interests inform the discussion—Ps 119:61 helps secure the meaning "cord, band" for all five anomalous forms. If *ḥevlê* in v. 61 can refer to a troop or a covey, it can do so in the four death/Sheol passages as well. The second meaning disappears altogether, and with it the force of the citation in Acts 2:24. This is Rashi's explanation, who translates, "bands of wicked men plunder me."[17]

Yet even here, the larger mediaeval Hebrew commentary tradition preserves the double meaning. This is clear in Qimḥi's explanation of v 61: "It was as though they plundered my soul with their intense antagonism toward me and the pains and agonies that they inflicted upon me. Nevertheless, I did not forget Your Torah."[18] The words "pains and agonies" show that Qimḥi recognizes in the MT's *ḥevlê* the word "pangs," and does not give to it the meaning "band, company."

This leaves the question of why English translations of our four texts render "cords," against the /e/-vocalization of the Masoretic Text. Even though the Hebrew reads "pangs of death," English translations continue to render, "cords of death." The Hebrew text seems to contain the second meaning, while our translations provide only the first.

One reason could be that the Targum's resistance to the masoretic vocalization remained alive in Rashi, whose influence in the KJV has been widely recognized. Of course, there is no need for polemic interests to operate in the KJV–NRSV tradition, but the translation "pangs of death," without a clear sense of the double reading, would be confus-

---

(Philadelphia: Jewish Publication Society, 1979).

17. סיעות רשעים שלוני, citing Gen 49:27 for the meaning "plunder."

18. A. J. Rosenberg, *Tehellim/Psalms,* Mikraoth Gedoloth 3 (New York: Judaica Press, 1991) 462.

ing, and Rashi's interpretation of these texts entered many reformation and renaissance interpreters. For example, Luther translated our Text #1, "Der höllen Band umfiengen mich," "the hellish band surrounded me."[19] I checked half a dozen seventeenth-century lexicons, all of which accept this meaning for *hevel* in these passages. The Targum becomes the main stream of interpretation, at least until Gesenius, who clearly turns away from rabbinic tradition.[20] It is found today in the REB, "The wicked *in crowds* close round me, but I do not forget your law."

But there are two losses in this development. One is in the reversal of the customary relationship between form and meaning. Ordinarily a word's grammatical form is a guide to its meaning; morphology guides, maybe even supplies, the sense. In disregarding the grammatical form of the word *hevlê* in these four texts, we see the perilous triumph of sense over morphology.

And the other is in the disappearance of a particular biblical witness to faith in the resurrection of the dead. The doctrine itself is not in jeopardy, for it is taught clearly in the New Testament and is supported by intimations in the Old Testament and by documents of the intertestamental period. The "binds/births" paronomasia is not the source of the doctrine, but a witty assertion of it. Still, any who see or feel the coils of death can only be grateful for the holy optimism that looks for a re-created suppleness where the natural eye sees only a final immobility.

And so I return to my wish that the hopeful outlook on death implicit in the paronomasia of this essay still be given the right to be heard. I can use its hope while I wait. That's waiting for the mailman, of course, with his last letter. But even more for the cry, "Go ye out to meet Him."

19. In Sebastian Schmidt, *In Librum Priorem Samuelis, Commentarius* (Argentorati [Strassbourg]: Spoor, 1687) 993.

20. For example, in his first edition (1810) he takes note of the masoretic role in vocalizing our five passages with /e/ instead of the expected /a/; but in the 1815 printing—not even a second edition—he drops the reference, forever. In subsequent editions he begins to provide classical explanations and parallels instead.

PART TWO

Studies *in* History *and* Theory

8

Leviticus as Christian Scripture

Ephraim Radner

MY DAUGHTER BEGAN A DEVOTIONAL DISCIPLINE WHEN SHE WAS twelve, one of reading a chapter of the Bible every night, starting with Genesis. She had reached the First Book of Kings before I learned what she was up to. By the time my son decided to follow his older sister's suit, however, I was more on target; and I tried to make sure that I asked him about what he was reading as he went along. "I'm starting Leviticus," he told me one day. He was eleven at the time. I found myself saying to him, without even thinking, "You might want to skim the thing—you know, just a little here and there, and then move on to the next book." My instinct was to protect him from the Leviticus' *longeurs*. I didn't want him discouraged so early on in his discipline, which after all, is meant to edify, not drag down into boredom. His response, however, was quick and decisive: "I must read every word," he said nobly. "It's the Bible!" But to what end? I found myself wondering.

Both reactions—my instinct to free him from the burden of the book, and his to press on through it in every detail—are bound to the character of Leviticus. Origen sums up this inner dynamic:

> It you read people passages from the divine books that are good and clear, they will hear them with great joy. . . . But provide someone a reading from Leviticus, and at once the listener will gag and push it away as if it were some bizarre food. He came, after all, to learn how to honor God, to taken in the teachings that concern justice and piety. But instead he is now hearing about the ritual of burnt sacrifices!

It's a deadly thing, though, that people come to church and
hear readings about sacrificial rites, the observance of Sabbaths and
such things, and then are put off, saying, 'why do we have to hear
these things read in church? What good does it do us to listen to
the Jewish laws and to the observances of a despised people? It's the
Jews' business; let them deal with it!' But [we must rather] begin
from the principle that 'the Law is spiritual' if we are to understand
and explain all the lessons that are read.

For my part, and because I believe what my Lord Jesus Christ
has said, I think that there is not a 'jot or tittle' in the Law and the
Prophets (Mt. 5:18) that does not contain a mystery."[1]

Yes, Christians are put off by Leviticus; but still, there is something divine
to be received within its words.

Despite Origen's hopes, however, Leviticus is today probably among
the least read books of Scripture, by Christians anyway. It is rarely quoted
in the New Testament itself, there being, on one count, only nine direct ci-
tations. But one verse—loving one's neighbor as oneself (Lev 19:18; Mark
12:31)—stands as a centerpiece within Jesus' teaching about the Law, and
has thereby proved enormously influential within discussions of Christian
moral teaching. Furthermore, the sacrificial cult described in Leviticus
provides the major framework for at least one New Testament writing,
the Letter to the Hebrews. In the contemporary ecclesial culture wars,
Leviticus has taken on a special, almost emblematic prominence, standing
as a kind of dark bogey-man, throwing up poorly-understood but looming
injunctions against certain forms of sexual behavior. These prohibitions,
in turn, are tarred by association with a host of other Levitical attitudes
we have otherwise long left behind. This detail of historical experience
has itself given rise to a specific kind of defense for ethical "development,"
dubbed the "shellfish argument" ("we eat shellfish, don't we? So why can't
we also do x or y that is prohibited by Leviticus?"). Thus, despite its alien
and unwelcoming character, Leviticus is a book that is hard to escape, even
though we feel it would be easier, for a lot of reasons, if we could. Our
ambivalence here, furthermore, probably ends up informing our attitudes
towards certain more central facets of the Christian faith. For the fact that
Leviticus hovers, unavoidably, over the whole discussion of the Cross of

1. Origen, *Homilies on Numbers*, 27.1; 7.1; *Homilies on Exodus*, 1.4. These passages can
be found in the Sources Chrétiennes edition of Origen's *Homélies sur le Lévitique* (Paris:
Cerf, 1981) 1:14, 36.

Christ, the "sacrifice" of our Lord and the ritual of our eucharistic remembrances, not to mention over the forms of our common life and relations, means also that these central elements of our faith are themselves tinged with the very tension and confusion we feel about Leviticus itself.

Critically, the historical line of commentary upon the book has followed a process wherein this ambivalence has harvested an alien fruit. Between Origen—the Church's earliest, and surely still greatest, interpreter of the book—and Jacob Milgrom, Jewish author of the present era's most expansive critical study of the book, the evolution of interpretation has moved in a distinctive direction: bit by bit the Christian sacrificial focus upon the book has narrowed through ever elaborated historical interest in the sociological details of ritual, to the point that the text's even potential Christian character has disappeared almost wholly. In its place, a vast and towering historical reconstruction of Israelite and Near Eastern social cultus has emerged as the book's residual substance, like a voracious jungle that has overgrown a long-lost human dump, and through which readers must move either as painstaking botanists or cruel clearers of the forest, simply to reach the grim detritus of the text itself. Squeezed out completely in this history has been the divinely created and desired breadth of the world itself that the text was designed to comprehend and lay out to view within the context of redemption.

This trajectory of Christian commentary is little more than the outworking of the problem Origen had already noted with respect to Leviticus' place in popular perception, even in the early Church. While the efforts of Christian theologians of his era and after to respond to the range of Manichaean-like rejections of the Old Testament were largely successful, at least theoretically, Leviticus itself always proved an intransigently difficult case in the concrete. Origen's pioneering exegesis, both as a whole and with respect to Leviticus in particular, was a deliberate response to the widespread sense in the Church that the book was both too hard to parse and finally irrelevant (possibly even hostile) to Christian concerns. And his methods in this regard sought to open the details—the jots and tittles—of the book to the broad range of divine action and purpose in the world of creation and history as a whole. He did this through the use of what he called "spiritual" reading. The complexity of the text's details, from this perspective, corresponded to the almost profligate character of God's all-encompassing work in creation and redemption, and the Christian reader's vocation and privilege was to uncover and engage these details. In this,

Origen's approach was in tune with developing Rabbinic methods of interpretation, themselves mostly marginalized in today's reading of Leviticus among most Jews, although in each case—Christian "spiritual exegesis" and Rabbinic commentary like the *Rabboth*—there has been recently a minor renewal of interest among historical scholars.[2]

The fact that Leviticus' only substantial presence in the New Testament—but what a presence!—is given in the Letter to the Hebrews, of course, meant that, for Origen and all subsequent serious Christian interpreters of the book, Leviticus' "spiritual" reference would be primarily bound to the body and acts of Jesus as the Son of God. More than any other Old Testament writing, Leviticus demanded of the Christian exegete a figural reading, the theologically comprehensive character of which laid the foundations for the whole theory of Scriptural figuration itself from a Christian viewpoint. The reality of the Law as a "shadow" (Heb 10:1), and of particular sacrifices as "images" of some "heavenly pattern" (Heb 9:23), that is given its substantive appearance in the fleshly person and sacrificial history of Jesus (Heb 10:20), located the entire Old Testament in a relation of meaning and purpose that was novel and peculiar, certainly in reference to Jewish exegetical precedents for spiritual reading like Philo's. It is one thing to say that the letter of the text indicated some higher spiritual truth; it is quite another to identify that truth as Jesus, the Christ. Furthermore, by wrapping Leviticus up, as it were, in Jesus—"Sacrifice and offering thou wouldest not, but a body hast thou prepared me" (Heb 10:5/Ps 40:6)—Jesus himself was interpretively given over to all the details of that book's (and the Old Testament's) wide reach. This converse effect of the early Church's figural connection between Jesus and the Old Testament text is even less appreciated today than is the first. For if it is difficult to find Leviticus's meaning and purpose lodged in the body of Christ, it is even more difficult to find the meaning and purpose—the form—of Jesus expanded and explicated by the rich details of Leviticus. Indeed, the loss

2. See the overview by Robert L. Wilken, "Leviticus as a Book of the Church," comparing Origen and the *Vayikra Rabbah* on Leviticus, in *Consensus* 23:1 (1997) 7–19. It has been argued, e.g. by Jacob Neusner, that *Vayikra* or *Leviticus Rabbah*, to which I shall refer frequently, marks a dramatic re-orientation of Rabbinic reflection on Scripture, taking Scripture more seriously as a self-determining authority, as opposed to using it as a store of proof-texts for Mishnaic legal commentary. This evaluation certainly places the *Leviticus Rabbah* (whose dating is perhaps a good four hundred years after Origen, though based on much earlier material) in analogy with Origen's own dramatic re-appropriation of Scripture.

of the figural connection at its base has resulted in the squeezing out of the world from Jesus himself. Jesus is a "thinner" figure in contemporary understanding than in the dense personal reality he represented for someone like Origen, in part because a book like Leviticus in particular no longer traces the outlines of his being.

Perhaps the last modern interpreter to engage this density most fully (though only as a hope left unrealized by his death) was Pascal. For Pascal, the problem with the Old Testament and with a book like Leviticus especially, was not its seeming "irrelevance" to Christians. The book might well be construed in a (subjectively) "relevant" fashion, but what did that matter if the scope of relevance itself was spiritually deformed? The problem Leviticus, and the whole "law and the sacrifices" was the fact that its details, if taken or dismissed in their simple literal character, mirrored a kind of person whose "carnal" nature was more interested in a superficial life than in being subjected to the hard realities of selfless love for God. Scripture is *difficult*, Pascal insisted, and no more so than when we attempt to decipher the true meaning of the Law and the Sacrifices. If that difficulty is avoided—by simplifying literalisms which, through their embrace or rejection, dispense us from grappling with the Scripture's "obscurity"— then the full depth of God's character, work, and vocation in Christ will be pushed aside as well (cf. *Pensées*, Fragment 287). "Objections by atheists: 'But we have no light'" (Fragment 244);[3] that is, "none of this makes any sense, so why bother?" Scripture's own discussion of the sacrificial ceremonial, for instance, is filled with "contradictions," Pascal notes in a lengthy fragment from his unfinished defense of Christianity: in some places (like Leviticus), Scripture says the sacrifices are "pleasing" to God; in others they are said to be "displeasing" to God (as in some of the Psalms and Prophets). Yet both cases, because they are Scripture speaking, are the "truth" itself. Only a "figurative" reading of the sacrifices, Pascal argues, can "reconcile" such a contradiction, not in a wooden sense, but by attaching each reality—the positive and negative character of the sacrificial ritual in the eyes of God—to the full historical ministry of Jesus whose own life in the Father's purposes is marked by a deep "obscurity" that expresses the profound reality of created human nature and redemption (see Fragments 257–260).

---

3. Blaise Pascal, *Pensées*, trans. A. J. Krailsheimer (London: Penguin, 1966).

How does this happen? Because Scripture is the living word of God, our engagement with its reading represents God working with us. And the very details of Scripture, as they exercise our understanding and care, are therefore instruments of the primary mission of God in our souls. Leviticus—even before it is examined—must be assumed to be a means by which the truth of God is exposed to us for our eternal destiny. Now the whole of reality comprises two foundational truths, according to Pascal: the "redemptive" love of God, and the "corruption" of human life and nature. If, that is, Leviticus stands upon a contradiction regarding the character of its referents—e.g., opposing views of sacrifice—it can only be because these referents themselves must be examined as caught up within and as markers of the contradiction itself. It is the holding together and exposing of these two truths of redemption and corruption simultaneously that the Christian faith represents and that Jesus himself embodies in the flesh of space and time, and that Scripture's writing and reading enacts.

But just in this, the entire world and the world's history is implicated: what it means to traverse the centuries, to encounter creation, to navigate the challenges of heart and being, to be confronted by God and to be taken up by God, is here included. "He is a God who makes [human beings] inwardly aware of their wretchedness and his infinite mercy; who unites himself with them in the depths of their soul: who fills it with humility, joy, confidence and love: who makes them incapable of having any other end but him" (Fragment 449). And Scriptural figuration itself somehow enacts the sweep of this historical and metaphysical reality in its very challenge. The "obscurity" of the Levitical ceremonial, for example, works both a cosmic light and darkness upon the reader that finds its full substance (and actual origin) in the "humiliated" Christ who expresses the divine love that is Scripture's only purpose to articulate: "If there were no obscurity man would not feel his corruption: if there were no light man could not hope for a cure. Thus it is not only right but useful for us that God should be partly concealed and partly revealed, since it is equally dangerous for man to know God without knowing his own wretchedness as to know his wretchedness without knowing God" (Fragment 446; see also 220; 268).

The whole Scriptures thus work as a concurrent "blinding" and "enlightening," according to Jesus' own explanation of his parabolic teaching on the basis of prophetic speech in general (cf. Fragments 332–336; Mark 4:12 and Isa 6:9). "'The disciples came and said to him, 'Why do you speak to them in parables?' . . . 'Because seeing, they see not; and hearing they hear not, neither do they understand, and in them is fulfilled the prophecy of Isaiah'" (Matt 13:10, 13). The centrality of this form of speech within the ministry of the Son as whole marks figuration as a supreme instrument of divine "love," by which (as Augustine insisted) all readings of Scripture are to be judged: "Look at all the prescribed ceremonies and all the commandments not [explicitly] directed towards charity, and it will be seen that they are figurative. . . . Everything which does not lead to charity is figurative. The whole object of Scripture is charity" (Fragments 267, 270). And this charity, encompassed by the exfoliating figurative expositions of the Scriptural text, takes in the world: "God diversified this single precept of charity," Pascal concludes, so that whole of creation and our "curious" minds could be comprehended into its referential reach. And this is only because the "precept" and its Scriptural multiplication derives from the fact that "the world exists only through Christ" and "Jesus Christ is the object of al things, the centre towards which all things tend. Whoever knows him knows the reason for everything" (Fragment 449). Although the forms for reading Leviticus are not given in advance, we therefore know that *any* proper Christian reading of the text will somehow detail the redemptive work of the humiliated Christ upon the broken hearts of human beings and of the whole created order. "Figural" reading is the name we give to the outworking of this "somehow."

Pascal's peculiar Augustinian anthropology notwithstanding, the foundation for his approach to Leviticus was both traditional and traditionally expansive, in the line of Origen's early direction.

> The letter is seen just like the flesh [of the Incarnate Word], but hidden inside of it is the spiritual sense that is grasped like [his] divinity. This is what we shall find as we peruse the book of Leviticus, with all of its descriptions of sacrificial rites, its diverse offerings, and the ministries of its priests. These are all things that, according to their letter—which is like the flesh of the Word of God and the clothing of his divinity—both the worthy and the unworthy can apprehend and understand. But "happy are the eyes" [Luke 10:23] that see the divine Spirit hidden within, beneath the veil of the letter; and happy are those who apply to this hearing the pure ears of the inner man. If not, they shall clearly perceive in these words "the letter that kills" [2 Cor 3:6]. (*Homily on Leviticus* 1.1)

For Origen, as for Pascal, the incarnational image here is more than a metaphor: the figural meaning of the text represents and encloses the whole history of God's work with the world, the movement of the Logos in creation, judgment, and redemption, and the movement of the human soul within this larger current of divine work. As students of Origen have pointed out, his "method" of spiritual exegesis—whether considered in its two-fold scheme of letter and spirit, or in its more elaborate tri-fold scheme of "history, morality, and mystery"—is less the pursuit of a formal exercise than it is an engagement with a "word" that is understood to be intrinsically reflective of the full historical work of the Spirit that animates it. We are called to read the Scripture as participants in a divine economy through which the meanings of material realities—worldly and written—are given in these realities' disclosure of divine life.[4] The full range, therefore, of Levitical referents reflects the creative breadth of the Logos himself, in his Spirit-led mission from the foundation of the world and into the Church's life as bound to the Incarnate One's body.

Origen was not the only reader of Leviticus in the early Church, but he was by far the most powerful. Even while other theologians, from Tertullian through Augustine, might approach the book most frequently in terms of its place within the *history* of God's pedagogy of Israel, when it came to the actual meaning of specific texts. Origen's spiritual exegesis dominated. And medieval exegesis tended to follow, rather than build upon this tradition. Origen's influence proved decisive through the sixteenth century, either directly or through intermediaries like Hesychius of Jerusalem, and then later compilations like the *Glossa Ordinaria*. There are in fact more extant manuscript witnesses to Origen's *Homilies on Leviticus,* in Rufinus's Latin translation and paraphrase than to his other commentaries on the Hexateuch, for the book itself provided the clearest application of the exegetical method based on multiple senses that was central to medieval reading. Furthermore, the elaborated evolution of the Western Church's sacramental culture proved a fertile parallel, figurally and in its own significating right, to the cult of ancient Israel, and the book of Leviticus proved a sturdy imagistic bulwark in this regard to liturgical life. To a real extent, this actually tended towards the desiccation of Leviticus' exegesis, as the book's objects and referents were increasingly given rote explications that simply followed the fittings of current ecclesial practice.

4. See Marcel Borret's careful Introduction to Origen's *Homélies sur le Lévitique* (Paris: Cerf, 1981) 1:22–34.

This observation is important. Even Origen's homilies, especially if read in sequence as a whole, can become wearisome in their unrelenting insistence upon the spiritual referents of the text. But it is crucial to note the character of this insistence, for its limitations lie less in the motive than in the pinched unidirectional dynamic of his interpretations, that jump almost immediately, over and over again, to the New Testament texts dealing with levels of virtue and vice, and the ascetic soteriology with which he tended to work, however richly. By the Middle Ages, this habit had made Leviticus, in many instances, no more than a handbook of Christian tropes, that did little, in fact, to open the Scriptural text to the fullness of the incarnational implications Origen himself held as foundational. Curiously, a better place to see this Scriptural opening and even incarnational implication is in Jewish exegesis, as it developed its midrashic methods and traditions, ones still employed especially in the orthodox hassidic interpretive communities, and founded on the reality that the Temple's disappearance redirected the localized cultic laws towards other referents.[5] The *Leviticus Rabbah*, as I mentioned earlier, represents a critical, indeed essential, fertile, and in many ways, easily adapted exegetical orientation for Christian reading of Leviticus in particular. While the *Rabbah* assumes wider referents—"spiritual" in a broad sense—for the objects of the text, these are never reduced to what become the free-floating emblematic catalogues of the Middle Ages. Rather, these referents are always discerned through the traversing of the history of Israel and its Scriptural persons, from Adam and Cain to Abraham and into the times of the Kingdoms. If, for instance, a purificatory rite is being examined, its meaning is derived only through a dynamic sifting of the lives and intra-textual discussions, as it were, of Abraham and David, of Israel and Persia, of Isaiah and Moses, as their own lives engage the realities of sin and forgiveness. Each speaks to the other, with Leviticus as a kind of narrative forum. Obviously, the "chronological" character of narrative here is drastically loosened, but the narrative and temporal moorings of Leviticus are heightened, not lessened, through its words being suffused by the history of Israel and its people. And this, frankly, is a greater witness to Word made Flesh—because the

---

5. Cf. the Babylonian Talmud, *Megillah* 31b: "Abraham said, '. . . but when [the Temple] does not [exist], what will become of [the sacrifices] then?' God said, 'I have appointed for them the chapters about the sacrifices: whenever they read them, I will reckon it to them as they had brought the offerings before me, and I will forgive them their sins.'" The "reading" here became associated as well with prayer and suffering.

landscape of Scripture is always inhabited by a people with whom God is engaged—than are the almost abstracted symbolizations that end up dominating Christian exegesis of Leviticus, and that, for all the Reformers' rejection of their fabricated particularity, still inform the Protestant reduction of the Old Testament's cultic and even legal material to contemporized moral allegory.

Yet even despite the drift into leaden symbolism, the medieval tradition nonetheless managed to keep the "letter" of Leviticus from turning into a mere husk. For concurrent with the formalizing of typological and allegorical readings of the book, Christian exegetes maintained a strong and continued conviction that the interplay between literal object and spiritual meaning within the text was a crucial sign of the outworking of *God's* acts of judgment and mercy in the history of the world and of the human soul. The *Glossa,* citing Hesychius, introduces Leviticus as the place where God exposes humankind to the "good law" of life and the "bad law" of death, spoken of in Ezekiel 20:11 and 20, and here given in the single words of the text to the Spirit-led or abandoned individual and people.[6] The whole drama of salvation is played out in the text and the text's actual reception, as the figural interpretive enterprise engages the hearts and hopes of the book's readers. This was exactly the view Pascal embraced with a passion:

> Each man finds in these promises [of the Law and sacrifices] what lies in the depths of his own heart; either temporal or spiritual blessings, God or creatures . . . [and] those who are looking for God find him, without any contradictions, and find that they are bidden to love God alone and that a Messiah did come at the time foretold to bring them the blessings for which they ask. (Fragment 503)

And finding God, they find, turning back to the letter of the text, all the creatures of God as they are properly to be loved.

That Leviticus contained the "world" was a Jewish conviction and, retrospectively rightly ordered in Christ, was a Christian assumption derived from Origen's incarnational reading of the text. And still in the Middle Ages the assumption was elaborated so as to induce sometimes an almost joyful appropriation of the book's referents towards a celebration of creative blessing. Bede had early used Psalm 19's praise of the Law to

6. Patrilogia Latina 113:297.

explicate the order of the Pentateuch, with each book somehow illustrating a kind of historical progression from Natural Law through to the written and finally to the New Law of the Gospel. Within this schema, Bede suggested that Leviticus represented a kind of "clarifying" word on the distinctions of these contrasts, with God speaking to the movement from Nature to Christ. The call by God to Moses for ordering the offerings of the people that opens the book becomes, in this reading, the figure for the whole world's gathering in faith, and the animals and objects are each laid out in the text as embodied images of the evangelical work of drawing in the nations through time.[7] The reader of Leviticus, then, is asked to engage a kind of map, that traces the work of God in history, and whose apprehension provides a living structure to the actual life of the world in which the reader lives. Although attempts were made to render this kind of exegesis "methodical" in its ascetic exercise, with one "sense" of the text purportedly built upon another (literal first, then allegorical, then moral)[8] and following the progress of the soul's ascent to God, the actual practice of figural reading in its details strikes us as conspicuously unordered. Indeed, medieval commentary on a book like Leviticus appears like a random pile of symbols. But the coherence and relationship of the details is given, not so much in a methodological outline of reference, as in the underlying assumption that the book as a whole depicts the work of God in Christ on a cosmic scale, comprehensive enough to demand the wealth of detail figured in the book's verses. In this sense, the associative method of medieval exegesis, whereby images from the primary text are brought into relation with other parts of the Bible not out of a systematic logic but merely through linguistic concordance, is deliberately "arbitrary," from a human perspective. For it submits, first of all, the ordering of the figures to the initiative of the divine "letter," given as an array of scriptural articulation that is granted a kind of inherent verbal networking. And second, it assumes that the economy of Christ has pre-established these connections through the simple reality of his "subjecting all things to himself" (1 Cor 15:27f.). There is a power of divine gravity that directs the ordering of figuration, as a kind of magnetism of form.

---

7. PL 91:331ff.

8. See Borret's Introduction to Origen's *Homélies sur le Lévitique*, 25–34; cf. also Ellen Davis, *Wondrous Depth: Preaching the Old Testament* (Louisville: Westminster John Knox, 2005) 76–77.

The Letter to the Hebrews, in fact, locates the work of God depicted in Leviticus in the actual *body* of Christ. This underlying reality, grasped by Origen and made central in all subsequent Christian commentary, includes not only the more obvious sacrificial details of the book, but also the communal laws of Israel's familial and civic relationships, whose referents must ultimately extend to the Church as members of Christ. More broadly, the body of Christ in its personal and ecclesial aspects, is seen to be the vehicle by which all of creation as brought into the reconciling purpose of God (cf. Col. 1:15-20). Thus, it persists as the referent even of the disparate details of animal and plant existence that populate the text within its legal demarcations. The world-historical character of Hebrews' own exposition of the fate of Christ's body demanded such a sweep (Heb 1:1–3), and, at least through the seventeenth century, it still informed the reading of Leviticus in a crucial way, as something like Andrew Willet's elaborate commentary shows.[9] Just as the Son and the Father are "one" (John 10:30), and whoever "sees" the Son has "seen the Father" (John 12:45), so the divine will behind the Law of Leviticus finds its formal exposition within the body of the Son himself as it reorders the whole of creation.

While some modern commentaries, particularly of a traditional Protestant orientation, have maintained a strict figural reading of Leviticus' sacrificial images, applying them to aspects of a carefully articulated atonement theology, even these have long been cramped by a single doctrinal focus that reproduces, in its own way, the disembodied emblematic universe of medieval exegetes. Calvin's example, though more supple than his followers' approach, nonetheless shied away from all but the most prominent sacrificial metaphors for Christ, leaving most of the book useful only in terms of its depiction of and exhortation to self-disciplined obedience and the virtues attendant upon it.[10] Leviticus fell prey to the

9. Andrew Willet, *Hexapla in Leviticum that is, A six-fold commentarie upon the third booke of Moses* (London: Printed by Aug. Matthewes, for Robert Milbourne, at the signe of the Greyhound in Pauls Church-yard, 1631). Willet's (part of a series he completed on several books of Scripture) is an extremely useful and detailed compilation of exegetical arguments both from antiquity, as well as from a range commentators of his own era, including many Roman Catholic and Reformed ones. He refers regularly to Rashi as well, and despite his own Puritan Anglican convictions, treats most of his sources fairly if unimaginatively.

10. Since all the "ceremonial law" is fulfilled in Christ, their only value now is to show us how, in moral terms. to live now with Christ. Cf. his comment on Lev 3:1: the Israelites' obedience to the details of sacrifice teach us moral subjection to rule of Christ in terms of different virtues, like scrupulosity of devotion, thanksgiving, attentiveness, and so on.

general skepticism over figural readings that crept over the churches after the Reformation divisions, and its content quickly proved uninteresting to the growing doctrinal-historical approach to the Scriptures that took its place. At best, the book provided sensationalist fodder to skeptical opponents of Scriptural authority as a whole, as is still the case. By and large the book has fallen readily into the most marginalizing exercises of historical-critical inquiry. To be sure, by the end of the nineteenth century, Leviticus' consignment into the dustbin of "Judaic superstition" at the hands of Deist and rationalist polemics, was alleviated slightly by the rise of anthropological inquiry and the developing interest in comparative religion as a discipline. New insight into the character of "sacrifice" and "holiness" as more general elements of *human* religiosity provided Leviticus with a reburnished profile as a major literary example within the collection of data being assembled by scholars to plumb the depths of the religious psyche of humanity. At the same time, the book's place within the evolving theoretical frameworks of documentary criticism of the Bible was always important. But none of this did much to encourage the actual *reading* of Leviticus as a living word from God within the Christian Church, and the book continues to languish in the backwaters of last-ditch bible studies and in the initial rush of introductory Scripture courses.

This commentary takes its place within the course of the traditional reading of Leviticus that came to its end, at least as a living thing, in the early modern period. It is not a "history" of interpretation, but a theological reflection; and so it uses only a small number of prior readers, Christian and Jewish, more as types of understanding, prying open a hearing in the heart. It is a Christian reading, bound to the life of Church and her reality as the Body of Christ, but deeply informed by the Jewish discipline of treating the Scriptures as a still-inhabited universe. But because of this, it is a difficult reading, attempting to outline the obscurities, not the simplicities, that determine our calling as followers of one of whom "the world was not worthy" (Heb 11:38), though by whom the world was loved to the Son's own death (John 3:16). The reading of Leviticus, in this sense, is a "hard and narrow way" (Matt 7:14), it is a kind of discipleship, whereby our own hearts are exposed to the world's edges even as they are challenged and transformed by the world's Redeemer. This is a reading filled with images of "becoming," as the encounter of the text with Christ's world transforms all that is in it, text and world together. Things and objects "become" new; they do not only "stand for" one another. Well might we yearn for protection from such an encounter; but in this we would desire wrongly. If in fact "Jesus also suffered without the gate" (Heb 13:12), and in this showed forth the meaning of those beasts burnt outside the camp in Lev 4:21, so in the very act of apprehending such a truth with joy, we too "go forth unto him outside the camp" (Heb 13:13), we too follow.

If there is a movement that takes place in Leviticus—a movement discovered in its reading—it is not only the movement of the human soul as it is snared by the challenges of a spiritual text and taken to a new place of love. For this could only happen if there were a prior movement of the Spirit, one in which the Son of Man goes forth into the world, and through it and with it, "goes to the Father," and if this prior movement were the foundation of the text and its details. This is the great following we undertake, and through it, the hard reading of this book marks out the "good work of his will" (13:21).

9

Karl Barth on the *Imago Dei*

Typology and the Sensus Literalis *of Holy Scripture*

Craig A. Carter

IN THIS ESSAY, I WANT TO DO TWO THINGS. FIRST, I WANT TO SHOW THAT Barth understood the *sensus literalis* (the literal or plain sense) of Scripture as including the figurative or typological sense, not as a different meaning but as itself part of the literal meaning of the text and, second, I want to discuss the implications of Barth's approach to theological exegesis for contemporary theology. In order to accomplish these two goals, I first will sketch some of Barth's key hermeneutical convictions and then briefly describe his interpretation of the *imago dei* in Genesis 1–2. In doing so I hope to contribute to the debate over the validity of Barth's definition of the image in terms of the fact that God created humanity as male and female. If I have anything original to contribute to this debate, it is my contention that it is the typological interpretation of the human creature in terms of Israel and Jesus, which is developed in Barth's comments on Genesis 2 that is decisive for Barth's interpretation of Genesis 1:26–27. Then, I will offer some reflections on how Barth's approach to theological exegesis offers a way forward that avoids the twin dead ends of liberal and conservative versions of historicism. My view is that Barth's theological exegesis is a like a long, gentle rain on the dry, barren land of historical-critical exegesis and self-referential preaching in the modern Church. In Barth's theological exegesis we can discover, if we take the time to look carefully, a way of handling Scripture that could lead to a revival of preaching in which the life-giving Word of God can be heard by the church, that is preaching in which God speaks and acts to bless His people.

Barth's Theological Interpretation of Scripture

Part of the reason Barth seemed so out of step with both his liberal and conservative contemporaries on the issue of biblical interpretation, both in his early commentary on Romans and also in his *Church Dogmatics*, is that he worked in a different context than they did. He worked in the context of the historical tradition of scriptural interpretation in the Christian Church, not just in the modern context of university-based historical-critical scholarship. Although he was highly skilled in the scholarly study of the Bible, his real interest was in utilizing historical-critical studies in the service of theological exegesis for the sake of the Church and preaching. So, for Barth, the practice of historical-critical studies could never be an end in itself. His treatment of the meaning of the image of God in Genesis 1–2 is both scholarly and theologically insightful. He devotes nearly three hundred pages to a close reading of these two foundational chapters of Scripture.[1] While he interacts continuously with historical critics like Herrman Gunkel and Walther Zimmerli, he also considers the views of Augustine, Luther, and Calvin at every point. For Barth, modern historical-critical studies have not rendered the opinions of the church fathers and the reformers out of date. He found in their writings more of a serious concern for the true subject matter of the text than he found in the writings of the modern historicists. In fact, Barth's quarrel with nineteenth-century, liberal, Protestant higher criticism can be viewed as a disagreement about what the true subject matter of the text is and what effect the subject matter of the text ought to have on the interpretation of the Scriptures.

For Barth, the Bible is about God. Its subject matter is the true and living God who speaks and acts, not a projection of the human imagination or a reconstruction of human scientific investigation. This is what separates Barth from the liberal Protestant tradition and also, strange as it may seem, from the tradition of scholastic orthodoxy as well. Liberalism viewed the Bible as a record of human experiences of the Divine, while orthodoxy viewed it as an inerrant record of historical events. Although Barth readily agrees with liberalism that the Bible is a human book and should be studied using all available methods of historical-critical research,

---

1. Karl Barth, *Church Dogmatics III/1: The Doctrine of Creation*, edited by G. W. Bromiley and T. F. Torrance, translated by J. W. Edwards, O. Bussey and H. Knight (Edinburgh: T. & T. Clark, 1958) 42–329.

he refuses to see the Bible as *merely* a human book precisely because of that to which it points. For Barth, this is a human book unlike all other books because in it we hear a true witness to God's self-revelation culminating in Jesus Christ. And, although Barth readily agrees with orthodoxy that the Bible conveys the history of revelation, he denies that scientific history, apart from faith, is capable of discerning that to which the texts points. Scholastic orthodoxy constantly veers close to the edge of saying that what the text refers to is accessible to unaided human, scientific reason. To say this is to reduce the Divine to an aspect of the natural world that is open to scientific investigation and human control and to refuse to allow God to be transcendent and free. The undeniably noble intent is to deny a Gnostic division between God and the created order and to affirm that God can act and speak in history. Unfortunately, however, the effect is to overwhelm transcendence with immanence and to make human rational capacity to demonstrate truth the criteria for the reality or unreality of God's action in history. Despite its intention to preserve the transcendence and freedom of God, conservative historicism ends up encasing God within human experience in such a way that, just as in the liberal account of knowing God through human experience, God is reduced to, and encompassed within, the limits of the human, that is, within creaturely limitations.

For Barth, the text conveys not only the historical effects of God's action, but witnesses to God himself because God's being is in His act. The text itself is Barth's focus, as opposed to a reconstruction of what supposedly happened behind the text, to which the text allegedly refers, or the experience of the biblical author. Why? It is because, for Barth, the human speech of the prophets and apostles functions as a witness to Divine self revelation. Like Calvin, Barth relies on the inner testimony of the Holy Spirit to give us assurance that the Word of God is true and views God the Holy Spirit as working through the text. As he says:

> . . . if it is really the case that a reader of the biblical Scriptures is quite helpless in face of the problem of what these Scriptures say and intend and denote in respect of divine revelation, that he sees only an empty spot at the place to which the biblical writers point, then in a singular way this does set in relief the extraordinary nature of the content of what these writings say on the one hand, and on the other the state and status of the reader. But all that it actually proves is that there can be no question of a legitimate understanding of the Bible by this reader, that for the time being, i.e.,

until his relation to what is said in the Bible changes, this reader cannot be regarded as a serious reader and exegete. There can be no question of his exegesis being equally justified with one which is based upon the real substance of the Bible, divine revelation.[2]

Barth rejects natural theology, both in the form of human experience of God and also in the form of scientific history, as an adequate prism through which to filter revelation. The only way to know God is through theological exegesis of the Bible because the only way to know God is to know Him in His own self-revelation, His own being. For this reason, theology is only truly scientific when it seeks to hear the Word of God (which is the being of God in God's self-revelation) through exegesis of the text. Humility, attentiveness and patience are called for in engaging the Word of God because our only hope of encountering the sovereign God is divine grace. Revelation is always grace for Barth and the interpretation of the Bible is as much a spiritual, as an intellectual endeavor. This is why, for Barth, prayer is essential to correct interpretation.

Barth presented his *Church Dogmatics* as a summary of the biblical witness to revelation and attempted to do biblical, rather than systematic theology.[3] As Richard Burnet notes, "Anyone who has read Barth for very long knows that his entire theological enterprise stands or falls on the basis of exegesis."[4] Over and over again in Barth's writings we are urged to keep close to Scripture and he constantly expresses his displeasure with those who, in their haste to explain what the text must or cannot mean, are

2. Barth, *Church Dogmatics, I/1: The Doctrine of the Word of God*, 2d ed., edited by G. W. Bromiley and T. F. Torrance (Edinburgh: T. & T. Clark, 1975) 469.

3. Barth contrasts his approach to theology with "systematic theology" in the Foreword to the Torchbook Edition of Karl Barth, *Dogmatic in Outline* translated by G. T. Thomas (New York: Harper & Row, 1959). The original lectures in this book were given in the ruins of the University of Bonn in the summer of 1946. Barth defines systematic theology as "an edifice of thought, constructed on certain fundamental conceptions which are selected in accordance with a certain philosophy by a method which corresponds to these conceptions" (5). He says that theology cannot be done under the pressure of such a confinement and must be free to be directed by the witness of the Old and New Testaments. The reader should be careful not to read too much into my use of the term "biblical theology" at this point. I simply mean to draw the same contrast Barth does. It should be noted that not only is Barth not a systematic theologian in this sense, but many writers normally classified as systematic theologians, such as John Calvin, are not actually systematic theologians in this sense of the term either.

4. Richard Brunet, *Karl Barth's Theological Exegesis: The Hermeneutical Principles of the Römerbrief Period* (Grand Rapids: Eerdmans, 1991) 10.

unwilling simply to let Scripture have its say. Barth viewed the modern, historical critics as being too hasty with Scripture, too ready to impose modern assumptions on the text, too eager to bring their own questions to the text and not humble enough to sit quietly before the text until it disclosed its own concerns. He tried not to impose a system upon Scripture and then seek prooftexts for what is known in advance to be the case. Instead, he sought to develop a theology that organically arises out of the witness of the Bible and that reflects the shape, limits and preoccupations of the biblical witness, rather than the demands of logic or the prejudices of the culture.

Barth's exegesis has a dynamic quality, as well as a static center. There are two forces at work: one pulling Barth upward toward more daring readings of the text and another pulling him downward to more verbal and modest readings. Let me try to clarify where these two forces originate.[5] Barth refused to let the original intention of the original author in the original situation be the absolute limit of what the text is allowed to mean, which is to say that he rejected the imperial demand of historicism. He viewed the canonical context as the final, authoritative context in which the text must be interpreted. He also viewed Jesus Christ as the central theme and content of both Testaments. He allowed each Testament to bear its own witness and felt no need to race from the Old to the New Testament in order to make the exegesis "Christian" because he believed that Jesus Christ is as much the theme and message of the prophets of the Old Testament as he is the theme and message of the apostles of the New Testament. Barth's exegesis is thus dynamic and daring in its willingness to see Jesus Christ in the Old Testament. This is where historicism is inadequate because a text embedded in the Old Testament may now have meaning that goes far beyond what the original author could have envisioned or intended in the original situation.

However, Barth remains utterly committed to a literal reading of the text and rejects the reading into the Bible of foreign ideas, philosophical systems and so on. This commitment to a literal reading exerts a restraining force on his exegesis that balances the dynamic pull of Christological interpretation. But the literal sense cannot be reduced simply to the histor-

5. I want to acknowledge the work of Kathryn Greene-McCreight in her wonderful book, *Ad Litteram: How Augustine, Calvin and Barth Read the "Plain Sense" of Genesis 3–1,* Issues in Systematic Theology 5 (New York: Lang, 1999), as having been extremely helpful at this point and in general for this paper.

ical sense for Barth is convinced that Old Testament speaks *literally* about Jesus Christ. We are not free to read in anything we wish; but we are not historicists either. These are the two extremes Barth is concerned to avoid. The interpretation of the two-testament witness of the Holy Scriptures to Jesus the Christ, is guided by the Rule of Faith.

Faithful teachers throughout the history of the Church have interpreted the scriptures of the Old and New Testaments in accordance with the Rule of Faith. Brevard Childs, in his magisterial summary of the history of exegesis, *The Struggle to Understand Isaiah as Christian Scripture,*[6] has shown that the standard textbook polarity between the supposedly sober, literal approach of the Antiochenes versus the alleged allegorical excesses of the Alexandrians is vastly overstated. In actuality, both schools employed figurative methods of exegesis because both were committed to reading the Old Testament as Christian scripture. Childs also shows that the standard, textbook portrayal of Calvin as a precursor of the historical-critical method is overly simplistic. For Childs, as for Barth, the historicism of the Enlightenment, when it is permitted to elide the spiritual meaning of the text, represents a major break with historic Christian orthodoxy and, therefore, is utterly incompatible with the apostolic tradition. Attempts by liberals to reformulate theology as talk about human experience of the Divine and attempts by both liberals and conservatives to refocus theology on the historical events referred to by the text were strategies developed in response to the Enlightenment, which ultimately fail because they do not challenge its historicist presuppositions. The portrayal of the literalism of the Antiochenes and Calvin was an attempt to enlist them as early examples of historicism by first reducing the definition of the literal to the historical and nothing but the historical and then emphasizing their stress on the literal sense as defined in this way. The difference between pre-modern interpreters and Enlightenment interpreters is that most moderns hold that the literal is nothing more than the historical. This crucial assumption was not held by pre-modern interpreters. In modernity, any attempts to do figurative or spiritual exegesis are left to the department of homiletics and biblical scholars piously avert their eyes at such "homiletical embellishments." Thus, the theological interpretation of Scripture is disconnected from historical exegesis and a wedge is driven between the scholarly study of the Bible and the ecclesial proclamation of Scripture to the detriment

6. Brevard S. Childs, *The Struggle to Understand Isaiah as Christian Scripture* (Grand Rapids: Eerdmans, 2004).

of both. Is it any wonder that preaching and theology are both in such disarray today? Is this disconnect between church proclamation and serious study of the Bible not related to what R. R. Reno refers to evocatively as the Western Church lying "in ruins"?[7] I believe that the recovery of the meaning of the literal sense of Scripture as the two-testament witness to Jesus Christ, interpreted according to the Rule of Faith, is absolutely crucial to the survival of the Church. And this is one reason why Barth's theology is so important to us today.

We ought to be grateful to Barth and Childs for clarifying for us the difference between a set of historicist philosophical presuppositions, on the one hand, and a concern for the literal meaning of the text, on the other. Equipped with this fundamental and crucial distinction, we are able to see that Barth was completely consistent to reject historicism, while claiming to recognize the authority of the *sensus literalis* of the text and the priority of exegesis in doing theology, all the while reading the Old Testament figuratively as a witness to Jesus Christ. In the next section of this paper, I want to describe an example of Barth's exegesis, so that we can see concretely how it works.

Barth's Interpretation of the *Imago Dei* in Its Canonical Context

Barth develops his famous thesis, "creation is the external basis of the covenant; covenant is the internal meaning of creation" from a detailed exegesis of Genesis 1–2. In the first creation narrative (the P account in Genesis 1), he finds support for the thesis that creation is the external basis of the covenant.[8] In the second creation narrative (the J account in Genesis 2), he finds support for the thesis that covenant is the internal meaning of creation.[9] In the first creation narrative, we see creation as a grand epic sweep of divine creative power bringing into being everything in the cosmos, but culminating in the creation of humanity on the sixth day. The cosmos is created as a home for the human creature. In the second creation narrative, we have a focus on the Garden of Eden as the special environment created for the human creature and an unpacking of the meaning of

7. This is Russell R. Reno's term; see *In the Ruins of the Church: Sustaining Faith in an Age of Diminished Christianity* (Grand Rapids: Brazos, 2002).

8. Karl Barth, *Church Dogmatics III/1*, 94–227.

9. Ibid., 228–329.

humanity being created out of the dust of the earth. Whereas the climax of
the first narrative is the creation of humanity as male and female as rulers
of the creation in God's name and by His appointment, the climax of the
second narrative is the creation of humanity as male and female. The first
narrative thus prepares the scene for the unfolding of God's covenant of
grace; the second recounts the beginning of the unfolding of the covenant
of grace.

In his exegesis of Genesis 1:26 "Let us make man," Barth notes that
we have here a pregnant pause, a "divine soliloquy, a consultation"[10] before
God acts. He rejects the common interpretation of the plural reference
here as being to a heavenly council and notes that the natural sense of the
text is not that God consulted someone else or some others, who then
faded into the background as God alone performed His creative work.
Rather, it seems that whoever the "us" is participates in the creative act
jointly. Barth thinks that the author of the saga has felt it necessary to
emphasize at this crucial moment that God is not lonely and creating the
human creature as an antidote to his loneliness. Wishing to stay with the
literal meaning of the text he cautiously states:

> He is One, but He is not for that reason one thing. But this be-
> ing the case, He can become the Creator and therefore have a
> counterpart outside Himself without any contradiction with His
> own inner essence, but in confirmation and glorification of His
> own essence.[11]

Barth does not read in the whole doctrine of the Trinity as developed
in the Fourth century, but he interprets what the text says as implying
diversity within the Divine nature (a counterpart outside Himself but not
in "contradiction with His own inner essence") that is consistent with the
dogma of the Trinity. Barth interprets the words "in our likeness" to mean
that God is creating a being whose nature is decisively characterized by the
fact that "although it is created by God it is not a new nature to the extent
that it has a pattern in the nature of God Himself."[12] Barth sees the human
creature as a "genuine counterpart" and "copy" of the divine nature and
he views the plurality in the divine nature hinted at here as pictured in
the two sexes of the human creature. Here we must pause for a moment

10. Ibid., 182.
11. Ibid., 183.
12. Ibid., 183–84.

and consider objections to Barth's interpretation of the image. Most Old Testament scholars prefer the functional interpretation of the image in which the dominion given to the human pair in vv. 28–30 is taken as the definition of the image, rather than the sexual differentiation of the man and woman.[13] It is often argued that sexual differentiation does not distinguish humans from the animals, whereas dominion does. But Barth counters that we must see the image as that in the human creature which makes the human creature a genuine counterpart to God, that is, as that which enables the human creature to stand in an "I–Thou" relationship to God. As he puts it: "Neither heaven nor earth, water nor land, nor living creatures from plants upward to land animals, are a "Thou" whom God can confront as an "I," nor do they stand in an "I–Thou" relationship to one another, nor can they enter into such a relationship."[14] The point here is not simply that humans exist in two genders, but that each human, by virtue of being created for relationship (as demonstrated by the way the man and woman find companionship and partnership with one another in an "I–Thou" relationship) is a fitting counterpart for God and can enter into a personal relationship with God. What we are as male and female is what makes us personal and capable of relationships with one another and with God.

Humans are not created in the image of a Unitarian God as independent and self-sufficient single entities. In this sense, the human creature is created in the image of the Triune God. But Barth says in anticipation of his later exegesis of Genesis 2: "The fact that he was created and exists as male and female will also prove to be not only a copy and imitation of his Creator as such, but at the same time a type of the history of the covenant and salvation which will take place between him and His Creator."[15] So we need to turn to Barth's interpretation of the second creation narrative, which presents the creation of the human creature as the creation of the covenant partner of God. There is a dialectical relationship between Barth's exegesis of Genesis 1 and 2, which attempts to do justice to their canonical juxtaposition to one another.

---

13. See Nathan MacDonald, "The *Imago Dei* and Election: Reading Gen. 1:26–28 and Old Testament Scholarship With Karl Barth" (forthcoming in *The International Journal of Systematic Theology*). I wish to thank Dr. MacDonald for permission to quote from this fine article prior to its publication.

14. Barth, *Church Dogmatics* III/1 84 ,1.

15. Ibid., 186–87.

In a programmatic statement at the beginning of his interpretation of the second creation narrative, Barth says:

> The main interest now is not how creation promises, proclaims and prophesies the covenant, but how it prefigures and to that extent anticipates it without being identical with it; not how creation prepares the covenant, but how in doing so it is itself already a unique sign of the covenant and a true sacrament; not Jesus Christ as he is the goal, but Jesus Christ as the beginning . . . of creation.[16]

Barth notes the significance of the use of the two-fold name "*Yahweh Elohim*" in Genesis 2, which is not used in Genesis 1, and calls it a key to the "peculiar orientation" of this saga. He comments:

> The second creation saga embraces both the history of creation and that of the covenant, both the establishment of the law of God and the revelation of His mercy, both the foundation of the world and that of Israel, both man as such and man elected and called. This is the theological explanation of its peculiarity.[17]

Now, heeding the constraints of time and space, we press on to a consideration of Barth's comments on the creation of humanity as male and female in verses 2:18–25. We begin by noting Barth's contention that the "account of the creation of man as male and female now forms the climax of the whole."[18] The fact that Adam was created to cultivate the earth, that God formed him from the earth, that God planted and prepared the Garden with the two trees (2:4–17)—all this leads up to the creation of the human creature "in the basic form of all association and fellowship which is the essence of humanity."[19] We are asked to notice the thoughtful pause in v. 18 "It is not good for man to be alone, I will make a helpmeet suitable for him," which reminds us of the earlier pause at Genesis 1:26. The account that follows gives us an insider's glimpse into the inner meaning of creation itself.

For Barth, the key to understanding these verses is the cry of Adam when God brings the woman to him: "This is now bone of my bones, and flesh of my flesh" (v. 23). Here Adam does not so much make a choice to

16. Ibid., 232.
17. Ibid., 240.
18. Ibid., 288.
19. Ibid.

accept the woman as his partner as to recognize the reality, which confronts him. The account of the creation of the animals and God bringing them to Adam (vv. 19–20) may seem to interrupt the flow of the narrative, but actually it is mentioned to highlight the uniqueness of the partner created for the man. It was not, Barth comments, "a divine experiment which failed," as if God had hoped Adam would be content with a nice tiger or dog or whatever as his companion. No, the point was that Adam be enabled to "recognize, choose, and confirm the helpmeet ordained and created for him."[20] The author of the saga has not put the woman on the level of the animals by introducing her in this way, but exactly the opposite.

That Adam was caused to fall into a deep sleep, receive a mortal wound, be immediately healed and then be woken up means that he did not participate in the completion of his own creation. Barth elaborates:

> The completion of all creation described here, i.e., the completion of man by the creation of woman, is not only one secret but *the* secret, the heart of all the secrets of God the Creator. The whole inner basis of creation, God's whole covenant with man, which will later be established, realized, and fulfilled historically, is prefigured in this event, in the completing of man's emergence by the coming of woman to man.[21]

Why is this creation of humanity in the form of male and female so important? Barth notes the statement in v. 24 that the man and the woman were naked and were not ashamed. Barth links this frankly erotic statement to the Song of Songs,[22] in which we have a picture of the covenant between God and His people in its perfect, unbroken and joyful condition. It is no accident that the prophets of Israel described the relationship between Yahweh and Israel in terms of marriage and that Israel is always portrayed as an unfaithful wife, while Yahweh is portrayed as a faithful husband.[23] For Barth, "the covenant which is the prototype for human love and marriage is the covenant which in its historical reality was broken by Israel."[24] Barth stresses that we miss the meaning of the prophets if we understand what they said about Yahweh's love for Israel as if it were a mere symbol drawn

20. Ibid., 293.
21. Ibid., 295.
22. Ibid., 313.
23. Ibid., 315.
24. Ibid., 316.

from the erotic sphere. It would be more accurate (though still wrong) to say that human love is symbolic of Yahweh's covenant love! But Barth stresses that the Song of Songs is not an allegory. "It says exactly what it says. It is undoubtedly and unequivocally an erotic history. But it exists in this concrete context and cannot be detached from it."[25] What context does Barth mean? The canonical one, of course: "As an absolutely pure and holy erotic history it has a meaningful place in the Old Testament because its background and context is the history of the covenant."[26] Here Barth lets the other shoe drop: "On this basis it is comparatively easy to understand the message of the New Testament as the fulfillment of the Old. In this respect, the Old Testament awaits a fulfillment which is not apparent in the framework of its own message."[27]

Barth proceeds to give a Christian reading of Genesis 2:18–25 in which Ephesians 5:32 is seen as a commentary on it, and therefore, on the Song of Songs and the prophets as well. "This is a great mystery, but I speak concerning Christ and the church," says Paul. Why not man alone, asks Barth? He answers:

> In the wider context we may answer that it is because the man Jesus, the Son of God, whose earthly existence was envisaged at the creation of heaven and earth, and the Son of Man whose manifestation and work were envisaged in the election of Israel, was not to be alone; because in His own followers, in the Church which believes in Him, He was to have His counterpart . . . It was not apart from them but with them that He was the firstborn from the dead. And therefore it was not without but with them that He was already the firstborn of creation.[28]

The sleep of Adam, the mortal wound, the healing and waking are types of the death and resurrection of Jesus. As Adam gave himself (his rib) for the creation of the woman, Jesus gave his own body on the tree as the means of reconciliation of sinners to God. As Adam jubilantly exclaimed, "This is now bone of my bone . . . ," so the Church does not first recognize Jesus, but is first recognized by Jesus. The human creature, Israel, Jesus and the Church are all intertwined in the mind of God, and in God's self-

25. Ibid., 319.
26. Ibid.
27. Ibid.
28. Ibid., 321.

revelation, and in the witness to that revelation in the Holy Scriptures of the Old and New Testaments. Barth summarizes:

> When the Old Testament gives dignity to the sexual relationship, it has in view its prototype, the divine likeness of man as male and female which in the plan and election of God is primarily the relationship between Jesus and His Church, secondarily the relationship between Yahweh and Israel, and only finally—although very directly in view of its origin—the relationship between the sexes. It is because Jesus Christ and His Church are the internal basis of creation, and because Jesus Christ is again the basis of the election and call of Israel, that the relation between Yahweh and Israel can and must be described as an erotic relationship.[29]

Reflections on How Barth Helps Us Move Forward

Now I wish to make some observations about what has been going on here. In his exegesis of the second creation narrative, Barth has (like the Bible itself) essentially repeated himself from a different perspective, while adding to and complementing the meaning of the first creation narrative. In the second creation narrative, the human creature is interpreted as the covenant partner of God and as the type of Israel, which is in turn interpreted as the covenant partner of God and the type of Jesus Christ. Jesus Christ, as the covenant partner of God who faithfully discharges his covenant responsibilities perfectly, thus fulfills the election of Israel and therefore fulfills the election of the human creature as created by God to be the elect covenant partner of the Creator in the priestly and kingly work of governing creation under the ultimate rule of God. Jesus Christ is therefore the ultimate meaning of what it means to be human and therefore also of what it means to be in the image of God. In his exegesis of the first creation narrative, that is, in his interpretation of the human creature as a personal being capable of "I-Thou" relationships, Barth has given an interpretation of the image of God as consisting in precisely that which is necessary for the human creature to be what the second creation narrative (interpreted typologically) says the human creature is in terms of the covenant. In other words, the personal and relational interpretation of the image given by Barth in his exegesis of the first narrative serves as the basis for the specific calling of the human creature in the second narrative, just

29. Ibid., 322.

as the creation of the physical universe in the first narrative serves as the platform for the unfolding of the covenant typologically prefigured in the second. Those who criticize Barth for his interpretation of the image in sexual terms need to realize that what Barth is really up to is interpreting the meaning of the image of God in Genesis 1 in recognition of the fact that Genesis 1 and Genesis 2 have been placed side by side in the canonical Scriptures, with the first as the context for the second and the second as the explication of the meaning of the first. It is the canonical shape of Genesis (and the Torah and the Bible as a whole in that these are the first two chapters of the Torah and of the entire Bible), that enables Barth to interpret the meaning of the image as he does. As the opening chapters of the Bible, Genesis 1 and 2 must be interpreted in light of the subject matter of the Bible as a whole, which is Jesus Christ. Finally, it should be noted that Barth does not completely reject the rule of the human creature over creation as part of what it means for humans to be humans. But he does reject the impersonal rule of humans in favor of what we could call something like rule-in-relationship, that is, a rule over the earth in the name of, by permission of, and with accountability to God.[30]

This brings us to the question of what it means to "read into the text" something that is not "there." Everyone seems to accuse everyone else of doing this and yet everyone seems to do it, at least as viewed from certain vantage points. Has Barth read a meaning derived from the second creation narrative into the first creation narrative and therefore interpreted the image in relational terms, (that is, as humanity being created as male and female and thus fitted for "I-Thou" relationships and as analogous to the Trinitarian relations of the Father, Son and Holy Spirit), rather than functional terms (humanity being given responsibility for ruling creation)? One might be tempted to ask why it has to be either-or and that would be a fair question. But there is another issue and it is the propriety of interpreting the meaning of Genesis 1:26–28 in terms of what we learn from Genesis 2. How can we say that Barth's interpretation is what Genesis 1 *means*, when he freely admits that the canonical context supplies part of that meaning? Nathan MacDonald, in a fine paper on Barth's interpretation of the image, points out that Old Testament scholars generally prefer the functional interpretation and regard Barth's approach as bad exegesis because Barth, in the words

---

30. It should be noted here that, as Brueggemann points out, "of all the creatures in God's eight creative acts, God speaks only to human creatures"; Walter Brueggemann, *Genesis*, Interpretation (Atlanta: John Knox, 1982) 31.

of Phyllis Bird, "has advanced only a novel and arresting variation of the classical Trinitarian interpretation, an interpretation characterized by the distinctly modern concept of an 'I-Thou' relationship, which is foreign to the ancient writer's thought and intention"[31] MacDonald also quotes James Barr's judgment that the functional view is the most influential today and that ancient Near Eastern texts that speak of the king as the divine image and therefore the Divine representative on earth provide the background to the idea of the image. The Priestly writer, Barr contends, has picked up this idea and applied it to the whole of humanity.[32] The ironic thing about this procedure is that it opens the door for modern readers to read into the text modern ideas of democracy, human rights and equality, which thus makes the text "relevant." It also permits the modern reader to read into the text the content of Egyptian or Mesopotamian or Babylonian ideas that may or may not have been in the mind of the writer of the text, even though they were currently existing or historical ideas floating around in the cultural milieu of the ancient Near East.

So there are at least three possible ways that modern readers can read into the text. It could happen that modern readers read modern ideas of democracy and equality into the text by reading it as a royal ideology critique. It could happen that modern readers read into the text ideas that were in the ancient Near Eastern culture, but which did not actually influence the specific writer of this specific text. Or it could happen that readers read into the text concepts derived from other canonical texts which have a literary and typological connection to the text when the text is interpreted in its canonical context. And this is not even to begin to go into the range of possibilities created by the rise of postmodern theories of subjective interpretation. I would agree with the postmodernists, however, that no interpretation of Scripture is entirely objective and scientific in the sense dreamed of by eighteenth-century Enlightenment writers. In order to read some meaning out of the text, one has to read some meaning into the text. This will be disconcerting to liberal and conservative interpreters (mostly biblical scholars) who prize scholarly objectivity and have faith in the historical method. But the real question is: "What shall we read in?" And, from the perspective of Christian faith, it seems clear to me that there can only be one right answer. We ought to read texts in their canonical context

---

31. As quoted by MacDonald, "The *Imago Dei* and Election."

32. As quoted in ibid.

and the meaning of each text is what the text says when interpreted in its canonical context.

This is not to say that our interpretation is merely arbitrary. To say, as Barth does, that the proper context for understanding the meaning of Genesis 1:26–28 is Genesis 2, the tendency of the prophets of Israel to compare the relationship between Israel and Yahweh to a marriage, the Song of Songs and Ephesians 5, seems no more arbitrary to me than deciding that an Egyptian royal ideology, rather than a Babylonian creation myth, is the decisive background for interpreting the text or than finding the ideals of the French Revolution contained in a three thousand year old biblical text. This is not to say that all interpretations are purely arbitrary, any more than it is to say that interpretation can be purely objective. Biblical interpretation is better understood as an art rather than a science. Barth's approach recognizes the need for prayer and the leading of the Holy Spirit in interpretation. But is this recognition any more than empty pious talk? What, concretely, does it mean to pray and try to be led by the Spirit? Well, could it not be that part of what it means is to allow the Spirit-inspired, providentially-assembled canon of Scripture to constitute the decisive and final context in which biblical texts are interpreted?

What does one make of the kind of typological and canonical exegesis Barth gives us? Although I have called it a gentle rain on the dry, barren land of contemporary exegesis and preaching, I am sure that many others would say it is just all wet. We should ponder hard why this type of exegesis and preaching is not standard fare in our churches and what is the source of the opposition to it. We should ask whether or not the dominance of the historical method in the academy can really be justified in terms of scholarly objectivity as the only scientific method. We should ask ourselves if we really believe that the Bible is one book with one author and if we really are convinced that the apostles were right to see Jesus Christ as the meaning and fulfillment of the Hebrew Scriptures so that they are rightly to be called the Old Testament of our Lord and Saviour Jesus Christ. We should also ask hard questions of those in the academy and in the church who practice the historical method as if it alone were all that is needed to interpret the Bible in an adequate manner. We should ask whether or not it might not really be the case that without typological interpretation we may very well fail to discern the spiritual meaning of the Bible and thus fail to hear the living Word of the living God. That is the question Barth refuses to allow us to avoid.

10

From Keble to Gore

A Study of the Use of Scripture in the Oxford Movement and by the Lux Mundi Group

C. Brad Faught

THE HISTORY OF THE OXFORD MOVEMENT AND, TO A LESSER EXTENT, that of what is often seen as its successor, the *Lux Mundi* group, is well-ploughed ground. According to the most comprehensive bibliography of the former, for instance, something on the order of 7000 books and articles have been published on the subject.[1] Lest any reader think making this point intends a criticism of the apparent ubiquity of works on the Oxford Movement, the present writer too has contributed to this vast corpus.[2] Interestingly, however, while much has been written about its leading personalities and the intensity of the controversies they provoked, very little work has been done on the way in which the Oxford men—the Tractarians as they were called once the *Tracts for the Times* gained wide circulation in the early 1830s—viewed and handled Scripture. Of course, cardinal to Tractarian thinking was the exalted place of the church, a readily acknowledged elevated ecclesiology, which might at first glance suggest that the Tractarians were not much interested in taking a party stand over the use of Scripture, conceding such to the Evangelicals for whom it occupied an understandably preeminent place in their thinking.[3] But, it may

---

1. Lawrence N. Crumb, editor, *The Oxford Movement and Its Leaders: A Bibliography of Secondary and Lesser Primary Sources.* (Metuchen, NJ: Scarecrow, 1988). A supplement was published in 1993.

2. C. Brad Faught, *The Oxford Movement: A Thematic History of the Tractarians and Their Times* (University Park: Pennsylvania State University Press, 2003).

3. See Peter Toon, *Evangelical Theology, 1581–3381: A Response to Tractarianism* (London: Marshall, Morgan and Scott, 1979).

be argued, the Tractarian view of Scripture was of vital importance to the development of the Movement and in the hands of John Henry Newman, Edward Pusey, and John Keble especially an identifiable position can be discerned, which in this essay shall then be compared to that held by the Lux Mundi group, specifically its leading light, Charles Gore.

Let us begin not with Newman, however, as most studies of the Oxford Movement do, but rather with Pusey, the so-called 'hermit' of Christ Church. This sobriquet was given to Pusey in the 1840s when the early death of his wife and the controversies of the Oxford Movement had weighed on him heavily, consolidating an earlier move by him to live a semi-secluded life in Tom Quad. Twenty years before, however, he had been anything but hermetic; in fact, his later reputation as an arch-conservative and ritualist (the latter being something of a caricature) is belied by his studies in the academic groves of German higher criticism as a young biblical scholar in the 1820s.

As Colin Matthew points out in an article whose title captures accurately his too-critical view of Pusey, "Edward Bouverie Pusey: From Scholar to Tractarian," Oxford's future Regius Professor of Hebrew started in a much different place theologically than where he finished.[4] Beginning in 1825, Pusey spent the better part of two years in Germany, the result of which was the writing of the most important theological work of his youth. Called a *Historical enquiry into the probable causes of the rationalist character lately predominant in the Theology of Germany* (1828), it comprised a wide-ranging attempt to come to grips with the "work of the chief German universities"; that is, with what today is called historical-critical studies of the Bible.[5]

Pusey's apparent acceptance of some features of new-style Biblical criticism was short-lived, however. Upon his book's publication it was met with unfavorable reviews, especially that by Hugh James Rose, a future Tractarian, who charged Pusey with rationalism and a low view of the apostolic succession.[6] These criticisms were enough, it seems, to compel Pusey to back away from his German-inspired ruminations and return to the safer confines of the high churchmanship and the traditional view of

---

4. H. C. G. Matthew, "Edward Bouverie Pusey: From Scholar to Tractarian," *Journal of Theological Studies* 32 (1981) 101–24.

5. Ibid., 106. See, also, David Forrester, *Young Doctor Pusey: A Study in Development* (London: Mowbray, 1989) chap. 2.

6. Matthew, "Edward Bouverie Pusey, 111.

Scripture in which he had been born and bred. It was from this position in the early-mid 1830s, therefore, that Pusey chose to make common cause with the men of the nascent Oxford Movement.

Meanwhile, someone for whom Germany could never conceivably be attractive, John Keble, had quit Oxford altogether. After an impressive undergraduate career capped by a double first in mathematics and classics, he remained in Oxford as a fellow of and later tutor at Oriel College. But the hurly-burly of Oriel intellectual life, spearheaded by a group of self-consciously progressive dons nicknamed the Noetics, was completely unappealing to the retiring Keble and so he left the ancient university city in order to take up the duties of a rural parish priest. Reluctantly, he did allow himself to be elected Oxford's Professor of Poetry, a non-resident position, in 1831. But the conclusion of its five-year term coincided with his being instituted to the living of Hursley in Hampshire in 1836. And in these salubrious surroundings he remained until his death thirty years later in 1866, far from the Oriel Common Room that, according to Newman, had "stank with logic."[7]

That leaves Newman. While Keble and Pusey were shaped by rural high churchmanship—in the latter's case by his aristocratic social standing too[8]—Newman's upbringing was urban (London) and evangelical. His conversion experience as a fifteen-year-old schoolboy left a deep impression on him.[9] But his years at Oxford as both undergraduate and Oriel fellow began a spiritual journey that of course led to his embracing Roman Catholicism in 1845. By that time leadership of the Oxford Movement had passed already to Pusey who, despite his own reservations, would be synonymous with Anglo-Catholicism for the balance of the nineteenth century. By that time too, a Tractarian view of Scripture had become well established. What was that view, and how did it change in the hands of Charles Gore some half-century later?

Here, Keble and Pusey are most important, partly because of their own essential connection to the establishmentarianism of the Church of England, and partly because of Newman's singular spiritual and theological odyssey culminating in his departure for Rome. Keble was the epitome

7. John Henry Newman, *Apologia Pro Vita Sua*, ed. Martin J. Svaglic (Oxford: Clarendon, 1967) 11.

8. See Faught, *The Oxford Movement*, 106–7.

9. See Sheridan Gilley, *Newman and His Age*. (London: Darton, Longman and Todd, 1990) chap. 2.

of the anti-modernist, and in this respect at least was the antithesis of the early Pusey. As noted above, Keble had already left Oxford, doing so in 1823. His subsequent priestly ministry was almost entirely pastoral in vocational terms and this of course meant the preaching of hundreds of sermons to rural parishioners, a group who could not have been less informed or less concerned about the emergent controversies over the study of the Scriptures, emanating mainly as they were still from Germany. Keble, while keenly intelligent and entirely capable of an academic defense of the so-called "old fashioned" style of scriptural interpretation, was at pains to stay clear of it when preaching to his rural flock at Hursley. Of course that should not surprise anyone, but perhaps it does, because the Oxford Movement is invariably thought of as a passionate campaign replete with controversy. Such, however, was never to Keble's taste, a priest whose fundamental conviction was that the pulpit should not be used for polemical purposes, even less for displays of eloquence. Apparently, so dismayed was Keble over being told that he had preached a very fine sermon one week, that he intentionally preached a badly organized one the next.[10]

For "Gentle John" Keble, his view of Scripture was inherited mainly from his saintly father, also in Anglican holy orders, and from study of the Church Fathers, exemplified most clearly in his editing—along with Newman and Pusey—of *The Library of the Fathers* in the 1830s. The patristic figurative technique of typology made plain in the series—broadly defined as the method of interpreting scripture that sees in the Old Testament "types" that point toward Christ incarnate in the New—was under attack by the German school and the Tractarians, as one part of their counterattack against the so-called tenor of the times, responded to it with vigor.

Keble's own response to what he termed the "fashionable liberality" of the day came in various forms.[11] His July 1833 sermon on "National Apostasy," which has come to symbolize the beginning of the Oxford Movement, is his most famous broadside against a multi-lateral modernism, particularly as reflected in Church-State relations. Preached from the pulpit of St. Mary the Virgin, the University Church in Oxford, it was both a lamentation and a call to action. But from his own simpler pulpit

---

10. Charles S. Dessain, editor, *The Letters and Diaries of John Henry Newman* (Oxford: Clarendon, 1975) 27:371.

11. John Keble, *Sermons for the Christian Year*, edited by Maria Poggi Johnson (Grand Rapids: Eerdmans, 2004) 2.

in Hursley Church, week in and week out, a quieter voice was heard. Keble sought to impress upon his local parishioners, a group made up of tradesmen, farmers, laborers, farm wives, and children, the traditional typological meaning of Scripture. For example, "what I mean by a 'type of the Cross,'" he told his congregation one Sunday morning, "I mean some person or thing, so described in the Old Testament that the faithful people of God, when they should read or hear of it long afterwards, might be put in mind of the Cross."[12]

In more sophisticated terms, Keble made the same point in perhaps his most important contribution to the *Tracts for the Times*. His Tract 89, the penultimate number in the series, was published in 1840, just a year before the Bishop of Oxford, Richard Bagot, asked that the controversial series cease publication owing ultimately to Newman's explosive Tract 90 on whether or not the Church of England's Thirty-nine Articles could bear a Catholic interpretation. "On the Mysticism Attributed to the Early Fathers of the Church," is a tract in which Keble is keen to refute the new-style Biblical criticism. In it he champions patristic Scriptural exegesis, citing Origen in particular, arguing that its typological and spiritual elements do not eclipse or interfere with the literal sense.[13]

Keble's steady defense of traditional methods of scriptural interpretation were of a piece with his endorsement of the religious establishment and of broader Tory political principles altogether. Within the Oxford Movement itself, Keble acted as a kind of lighthouse figure, guiding those who were otherwise unsure of which direction to take. As it was remarked of him by Pusey's biographer and spiritual heir, Henry Parry Liddon: "when all else had been said and done, people would wait and see what came from Hursley before they made up their minds as to the path of duty."[14] One of those of course who looked to Keble for spiritual direction was Pusey himself, whose initial encounter with historical-critical methods had been tested and rejected and in 1834 he made common cause with the Tractarians by contributing his first effort to the *Tracts for the Times*,

---

12. Quoted in ibid., 12.

13. [John Keble], "On the Mysticism Attributed to the Early Fathers of the Church," *Tracts for the Times*, No. 89 (Oxford: James Parker, 1868). See, also, Ephraim Radner, "The Discrepancies of Two Ages: Thoughts on Keble's 'Mysticism of the Fathers,'" *The Anglican* 43 (2000) 10–15.

14. Quoted in Georgina Battiscombe, *John Keble: A Study in Limitations* (London: Constable, 1963) xvi.

Tract 18 on fasting. As effectively leader of the Tractarians after about 1841, and of the Anglo-Catholics later on, Pusey's position in the roil of mid-Victorian debates over Christianity was never more central than in the question of Scriptural interpretation.[15] In much of the history of the Victorian-era, questions of belief and unbelief predominate. But, as George P. Landow points out, "this focus has been particularly unfortunate since the first two-thirds of the nineteenth century saw a great, almost astonishing, revival of biblical typology, which left its firm impress upon Victorian literature, art, and thought."[16] Landow's comment could send this study profitably into all sorts of directions, but what is of primary concern here is Pusey and Scripture. And one of his formal forays into the area came in a series of lectures he gave at Oxford in Michaelmas term 1836. Apparently, just twenty-nine people attended his "Lectures on Types and Prophecies of the Old Testament," but among them were Newman and Isaac Williams, whose own position in the Oxford Movement was becoming increasingly important and who would provoke a firestorm of controversy over his position on the doctrine of reserve in communicating religious knowledge.[17]

Pusey's lectures were a culmination of a concentrated period of study and they were concerned primarily with forwarding the thesis that types, symbols, and sacramental actions carry within themselves the biblical revelation. Pusey's Old Testament exegesis is relentlessly christocentric.[18] To Pusey, the Church Fathers, especially Origen, had read the Scriptures in "the apostolic mode . . . they had Christ always in their thoughts, and so with the full persuasion that the whole of the Old Testament, the law, the prophets and the psalms, before of him, they read and understood of Christ therein. . . ."[19] This christology is consistent with the Tractarians' increasing emphasis on the incarnation and on Eucharistic fellowship, which

---

15. See Peter G. Cobb, "Leader of the Anglo-Catholics?" in *Pusey Rediscovered*, edited by Perry Butler (London: SPCK, 1983) 349–65.

16. George P. Landow, *Victorian Types Victorian Shadows: Biblical Typology in Victorian Literature, Art, and Thought* (London: Routledge & Kegan Paul, 1980) 3.

17. See Faught, *The Oxford Movement*, 51. Also, [Isaac Williams], "On Reserve in Communicating Religious Knowledge," *Tracts for the Times*, No. 80 (London: Rivingtons, 1837).

18. David Jasper, "Pusey's 'Lectures on Types and Prophecies of the Old Testament,'" in *Pusey Rediscovered*, 51–70.

19. Quoted in ibid., 64.

would become a defining feature of Pusey's thinking in the years ahead, and in a different way that of Charles Gore also.[20]

Pusey's voice was a loud and insistent one in this regard in mid-Victorian society. As Oxford's Regius Professor of Hebrew and Canon of Christ Church Cathedral, he could be counted upon to weigh into most religious controversies of the time. But on the issue of Scriptural interpretation none was more significant than that over the book of Daniel. In 1862–63, Pusey gave a series of nine lectures at Oxford, published the next year under the title, *Daniel the Prophet*. As he described it in the Preface, "the following lectures were planned, as my contribution against that tide of skepticism, which the publication of *Essays and Reviews* let loose upon the young and uninstructed."[21] His reference of course is to the series of seven essays published in 1860, which formed the basis for a public "Liberal Protestant Christianity," as described by some. Coming just one year after the seismic publication of Darwin's *On the Origin of Species*, *Essays and Reviews* was the controversial work of six Church of England clergymen and one layman.[22] Together, they sought to critique the whole of Christian theology and the Biblical record through the prized use of so-called "free inquiry." What Darwin had done for science, the "Seven Against Christ," as they were disparaged by their critics, would do for the Church of England, or so they thought.

Arguably, the most important of the seven essays, "On the Interpretation of Scripture," was that written by Benjamin Jowett. As master of Balliol College, Oxford, later in his career, Jowett saw himself as the creator of a generation of statesmen. And in shaping the early lives of Lord Curzon, Viceroy of India, and H. H. Asquith, Liberal prime minister, to name two noteworthy examples, he was not wrong. But in 1860 Jowett was just a don, albeit as Regius Professor of Greek, not an ordinary one. (He was also "monumentally rude": "What I don't know isn't knowledge" is the way a bit of undergraduate doggerel described his attitude.) In his essay, Jowett argued that the Bible ought to be read like any other book. The aim of its readers should be a recovery of the authors' original meaning within their own historical contexts. He implied that divine inspiration

20. See R. W. Franklin, "Pusey and Worship in Industrial Society," *Worship* 57 (1983) 386–412.

21. E. B. Pusey, *Daniel the Prophet: Nine Lectures*, 6th ed. (London: Rivingtons, 1880) iii.

22. See Victor Shea and William Whitla, editors, *Essays and Reviews: The 0681 Text and Its Reading* (Charlottesville: University of Virginia Press, 2001).

had nothing to do with the creative process. He praised the "higher" critics, mostly German, who were seeking to confirm the events narrated in the Bible from independent sources.

Upon reading *Essays and Reviews* Pusey was quick to point out that nothing Jowett or any of his co-writers had said was new: "Human inventiveness in things spiritual or unspiritual is very limited. It would be difficult probably to invent a new heresy. Objectors of old were as acute or more acute than those now; so that the ground was well-nigh exhausted."[23] But what was new—and shocking for many—was to have it said from within the Church of England itself. Accordingly, institutional reaction was swift. Led by Samuel Wilberforce, bishop of Oxford, *Essays and Reviews* was condemned officially. Indeed, in 1862, two of its writers, Rowland Williams and H. B. Wilson, were indicted for heresy in ecclesiastical court, although later judgment against them was overturned by the Judicial Committee of the Privy Council. Meanwhile, Pusey readied himself to enter the fray and did so in a concerted fashion with his lectures on the book of Daniel.

For Pusey, the Church's foundational doctrine of the inspiration of Scripture was at stake in this controversy. As for the focus of his counterblast against those who would doubt the veracity of revealed religion, Pusey observes, "I selected the book of Daniel, because unbelieving critics [including Williams] considered their attacks upon it to be one of their greatest triumphs. . . . Only they mistook the result of unbelief for the victory of criticism. They overlooked the historical fact that the disbelief had been antecedent to the criticism."[24] As Christopher Seitz holds, Pusey's work on Daniel, that is, his defense of the traditional sixth-century authorship of it, displays a concern for "text, church and world," every bit as acute as that found in what would later be called specialized "academic discourse."[25]

What of it? As noted earlier, Pusey's Daniel lectures were delivered at Oxford in 1862 and 63. They focused upon the predictive character of the book and the harmony it displayed with the rest of Scripture. Pusey maintained that, given the familiarity with the customs and history of the time, the author must have lived during the period of its traditional sixth-century composition. Moreover, and against Daniel's biblical critics, Pusey was certain that, as Henry Liddon, his biographer puts it, "the theology of

23. Pusey, *Daniel the Prophet*, iii.

24. Ibid., vi.

25. Christopher R. Seitz, *Figured Out: Typology and Providence in Christian Scripture* (Louisville: Westminster John Knox Press, 2001) 15.

Daniel was exactly what would be expected from a Jew living during the Babylonian captivity."[26]

For Pusey, the Daniel lectures were a tour de force of biblical scholarship. They were thorough, replete with great erudition, and demonstrative of considerable linguistic skill and familiarity with Semitic literature. They were summative of forty years of work as a biblical critic and theologian, and they served a strongly polemical purpose as encapsulating the traditional conservative position on the inspiration of Scripture. They were also the last stand against Biblical higher criticism of the original Tractarians. Keble, looking on from Hursley and not far removed from his coming death in 1866, was equally wrought up by what *Essays and Reviews* represented. "I can compare it," he wrote in a letter to a friend in the fall of 1860, "to nothing but the reputed action of a rattle-snake; the sound of the rattle is heard and understood, and yet the fascination continues. . . ."[27] Pusey's own death would come in 1882. He remained the acknowledged leader of the Tractarians' heirs, the Anglo-Catholics, until the end, but his commitment to a traditional hermeneutic was one that many of his co-religionists simply could not accept. And chief among them was Charles Gore, at that time vice-principal of Cuddesdon Theological College near Oxford.

Born in 1853 in the leafy London suburb of Wimbledon, Gore, like Pusey before him, was the son of aristocratic privilege: both of his parents came from titled families. He was educated at Harrow and by the time he matriculated as a scholar at Balliol College, Oxford in 1871 his Anglo-Catholicism was assured. At Balliol, Gore came under the strong influence of Jowett, among others. A fellowship at Trinity College followed his first class degree in 1875. In that year too Gore and some likeminded young Anglo-Catholics founded what they informally called the "Holy Party," one of whose aims became the development of a liberal Catholicism in contradistinction to the Anglo-Catholicism represented by Pusey and the old Tractarian tradition. None of that, however, really came into sharp relief until long after Gore's ordination with, in 1889, the publication of *Lux Mundi*, a volume of twelve essays by a group of Anglican churchmen who, in their view, were offering a sympathetic engagement with contemporary thought. Gore was the book's editor. Earlier, in 1883, he had been appointed principal of Pusey House, the chief memorial to its recently

26. Henry Parry Liddon, *Life of Edward Bouverie Pusey* (London: Longmans, Green & Co., 1897) 4:72.

27. Quoted in Battiscombe, *John Keble*, 326.

deceased namesake and a place of Anglican learning, teaching, and pastoral care for Oxford undergraduates. But while pleased to undertake the appointment, Gore made it clear to Henry Liddon that he would not be adhering to every point of doctrine that had been upheld by Dr. Pusey.[28] That note of dissent, however, apparently was not understood.

What this admission ultimately meant was later revealed in Gore's essay in the *Lux Mundi* volume, "The Inspiration of Holy Scripture." The essay captured Gore's essential thinking on the hermeneutical problem first made plain in England by his sometime mentor Jowett in *Essays and Reviews* almost thirty years before. His main purpose in writing the essay, Gore states, is to meet the attack of Biblical criticism. To do so, he continues, "we are removing great obstacles from the path to belief of many who certainly wish to believe, and do not exhibit any undue skepticism."[29] To his critics, however, who emerged immediately, Gore had made a disastrous accommodation with Liberal Christianity. Liddon, in particular, was shocked. "*Lux Mundi*," he stated, "is a proclamation of revolt against the spirit and principles of Dr. Pusey and Mr. Keble."[30] Uproar within the Church of England ensued, the main point at issue being Gore's declaration that "it is the test of the church's legitimate tenure that she can encourage free enquiry into her title-deeds."[31] Of course, controversy meant that the volume sold wildly: ten editions in the first year, three in one month alone, May of 1890. Gore had sent Liddon a copy in advance of publication in order to try and assuage what he assumed to be the coming criticism. But he did not retreat from his stated position, which in fact had been developing since the late 1870s, that "it is impossible in any way to withdraw the historical basis of Christianity from the freest and frankest criticism. If there exist persons who say, let the Old Testament be frankly criticized for it is not so important, but not the New Testament for it is vital, the claim must be utterly repudiated."[32]

Gore's distinction here is suggestive of his critical approach to interpreting Scripture. In his *Lux Mundi* essay he was bold in his interpreta-

---

28. Liddon, *Life of Pusey*, 53.

29. Charles Gore, "The Inspiration of Holy Scripture," in *Lux Mundi: A Series of Studies in the Religion of the Incarnation*, 15th ed. (London: Murray, 1909) 266.

30. Quoted in G. L. Prestige, *The Life of Charles Gore* (London: Heinemann, 1935) 105.

31. Gore, *Lux Mundi*, 239.

32. Quoted in Paul Avis, *Gore: Construction and Conflict* (Worthing: Churchman, 1988) 43–44.

tion of the Old Testament, but not so in his handling of the New. This bifurcation troubled him for the remainder of his life, one that saw him become one of the most important figures in the Victorian and Edwardian Church of England as both bishop and theologian. It spoke to the teleology of his critical method; that is, can the progress of criticism, once begun, be brought appropriately to a close? His full endorsement of the critical method had, it is clear and despite his protestations, not encompassed the New Testament, and because of this inconsistency contemporary modernists were dismayed. No less dismayed, but for the opposite reason, are some biblical scholars of the present day who see in Gore "emerging the lineaments of a position on scripture completely twentieth century."[33] Where Pusey and Keble saw Scripture as a unity, where they recognized intertestamental congruence, Gore sees gradualness. That is, the Old Testament is by definition imperfect and is to be succeeded by the perfection of the New. Gore's undergraduate-taught Hegelianism is at work here, as is a controversial appeal to what he called "kenosis," which defined the Incarnation as a "self-emptying of God to reveal himself under conditions of human nature and from the human point of view," and to the Creeds.[34] This "Religion of the Incarnation," the stated theme of *Lux Mundi*, and which included the view that Jesus's knowledge was limited, then becomes the means by which the Old Testament and its attendant hermeneutical problems might be overcome.

Kenosis for Gore was problematical then and remains so now. As representative of a willingness to jettison the traditional idea of a single, unified Christian Scripture, to see, as he put it, "the Old Testament to be imperfect," he had indeed departed from the teachings of Pusey. Having done so, there was little hope that Anglo-Catholicism would not follow its new leader into the acceptance of a new Scriptural hermeneutic, ultimately much more in line with the writers of *Essays and Reviews* than with Pusey, Keble, and the old Tractarian tradition. Accordingly, and within a generation, such a transition had been made. It prevails still.

---

33. Seitz, *Figured Out*, 18.
34. Gore, *Lux Mundi*, 264.

11

De Genesi ad litteram and the Galileo Case

Jennifer Hart Weed

Introduction

HERMENEUTICS PLAYED A CRUCIAL ROLE IN THE CONFLICT BETWEEN Galileo Galilei (1564–1642) and the Roman Catholic Church. Surprisingly, Galileo cited the patristic hermeneutic of St. Augustine of Hippo in his defense of his commitment to heliocentrism. It could be said that it was Augustine's hermeneutical principles that saved Galileo from excommunication or worse.

The conflict between Galileo and the Church was set in motion in 1543, when Nicholas Copernicus (1473–1543) published his work, *De Revolutionibus Orbium Caelestium*, in which he argued for a heliocentric universe.[1] The Church condemned this work in 1616 for the following reasons:

1. Heliocentrism conflicted with the geocentrism held by the Church.
2. The Church based their geocentrism on an interpretation of Scripture.
3. The Council of Trent decreed the Church as the authority with respect to Scriptural interpretation.[2]

---

1. Richard J. Blackwell, *Galileo, Bellarmine, and the Bible* (Notre Dame: University of Notre Dame Press, 1991) 5.
2. Ibid.

Galileo agreed with Copernicus and he argued that Copernicanism was not in conflict with Scripture.[3] In 1615, he wrote a "Letter to the Grand Duchess Christina," in which he cited several hermeneutical principles from Augustine's *De Genesi ad litteram*, a literal commentary on the first three chapters of the book of Genesis.[4] Augustine was also interested in defusing conflicts between science and Christianity, and so his hermeneutical principles were devised in order to balance the concerns of both. In what follows, I will outline some of those principles with a view to explaining how they assisted Galileo in his attempt to defuse the conflict between Copernicanism and the Church.[5] I will also give attention to those aspects of Augustine's thought that undermine Galileo's project, as well. Finally, I will conclude with a short discussion of the relationship between science and religion.

The Interpretive Principles

Restraint

Galileo begins his letter to the Grand Duchess by describing several professors who had attempted to discredit his scientific research in support of Copernicanism by quoting Scripture.[6] Presumably, these professors had argued that the Scripture taught geocentrism by quoting some passages in the Old Testament that seem to indicate that the earth is at rest while the sun orbits the earth.[7] They would have argued that since Scripture teaches geocentrism and since Scripture is never false, then the view of geocentrism must be true. In response to this argument from authority, Galileo cleverly cites an alternative argument from authority; the authority

---

3. Galileo Galilei, "Letter to the Grand Duchess Christina," in *Discoveries and Opinions of Galileo*, translated and edited by Stillman Drake (New York: Doubleday, 1957) 177.

4. Stillman Drake, *Discoveries and Opinions of Galileo* (New York: Doubleday, 1957) 145.

5. Ernan McMullen has an extensive discussion of Galileo's appropriation of Augustinian principles in his essay, "Galileo on Science and Scripture," in *The Cambridge Companion to Galileo*, edited by Peter Machamer (Cambridge: Cambridge University Press, 1998) 271–347. My first two principles are also discussed by McMullen, but my discussion diverges from his.

6. Galileo, "Letter," 175, 177.

7. Although Galileo doesn't cite these passages directly, Blackwell identifies several of them, including Psalm 104:5; 1 Chronicles 16:30; Genesis 1:17; and Joshua 10:12, in Blackwell, *Galileo*, 60, 65.

of St. Augustine, who advocates restraint when one interprets Scripture. Augustine writes,

> We should always observe that restraint that is proper to a devout
> and serious person and on an obscure question entertain no rash
> belief. Otherwise, if the evidence later reveals the explanation, we
> are likely to despise it because of our attachment to our error, even
> though this explanation may not be in any way opposed to the
> sacred writings of the Old or New Testament.[8]

In this passage, Augustine's concern is with the conjunction of Christian doctrine and scientific theory. He is worried that someone might claim that Christianity requires a particular scientific view, only to have that scientific view falsified conclusively. Such a falsification would prove embarrassing to Christianity and perhaps persuade some people to believe that Christianity is also false. So with respect to interpreting Scripture on "obscure" scientific matters, Augustine advocates restraint. One should be restrained with respect to the strength with which one adheres to a given interpretation that has scientific implications because new evidence might expose those scientific views and therefore that interpretation to be false.[9] He continues by offering the following example,

> It is often asked whether the bright luminaries of heaven are bodies
> only or whether they have spirits within them to rule them. . . .
> This problem is not easy to solve, but I believe that in the course of
> commenting on the text of Scripture occasions may present them-
> selves on which we may treat the matter according to the rules for
> interpreting Holy Scripture, presenting some conclusion that may
> be held, without perhaps demonstrating it as certain.[10]

According to Augustine, one can hold a scientific view on the basis of Scripture but one must do so with restraint and one must admit when

---

8. St. Augustine, *De Genesi ad litteram*, trans. John Hammond Taylor, SJ (New York: Newman, 1982) II.18.38. Since Galileo's quotations are imprecise and unreferenced in the original, I will cite the quotations from Augustine directly. See Galileo, "Letter," 176. The Latin text of Augustine is included in *Corpus Scriptorum Ecclesiasticorum Latinorum*, vol. 28, part 1.

9. Of course, this statement assumes that the Scripture communicates truth and can-not communicate falsehood. This principle will be discussed in the next section.

10. Augustine, *De Genesi* II.18.38. See Galileo, "Letter," 199.

the view in question lacks demonstration.[11] With respect to the "rules for interpreting Scripture," Augustine presupposes that some passages can be interpreted in more than one sense, such as literally and figuratively.[12] He also notes that there are at least three different genres of text in Scripture, each of which must be identified and interpreted accordingly,[13]

> Thus, (for example) it is handed down according to history, when there is taught what hath been written, or what hath been done; what not done, but only written as though it had been done. According to etiology, when it is shown for what cause any thing hath been done or said. According to analogy, when it is shown that the two Testaments, the Old and the New, are not contrary the one to the other. According to allegory, when it is taught that certain things which have been written are not to be taken in the letter, but are to be understood in a figure.[14]

Although Galileo fails to enumerate all of Augustine's rules for interpreting Scripture in the *Letter*, he cites the principle of restraint as an argument from authority. The professors who oppose Galileo are guilty of quoting Scripture in favour of their own scientific views, despite the fact that those ideas have been called into question by other scientific investigations. Instead of being dogmatic in advocating for their views, they should have followed Augustine's advice in holding the position with restraint since further evidence could come to light that could show those views, and consequently, their interpretation to be false.

The Harmonization of Scriptural Interpretation with Demonstration

The second interpretive principle that Galileo derives from Augustine is that one should harmonize a given Scriptural interpretation with a scien-

---

11. Augustine has in mind a particular view of demonstration, which I will explain in the next section.

12. Augustine, *De Genesi* I.19.38.

13. Henri de Lubac, SJ, *Medieval Exegesis*, vol. 1, trans. Mark Sebanc (Grand Rapids: Eerdmans, 1988) 124. De Lubac does not view etiology and analogy as separate senses. He also disagrees with the opinion that Augustine identifies history, etiology, analogy and allegory as four different senses of Scripture, see 123–27.

14. St. Augustine, "De Utilitate Credendi," in *Seventeen Short Treatises of St. Augustine, Bishop of Hippo*, trans. C. L. Cornish and H. Browne (Oxford: Parker, 1847) 5.

tific demonstration. Augustine argues that a Scriptural interpretation can be falsified by a demonstrated truth that contradicts that interpretation,

> When they are able, from reliable evidence, to prove some fact of physical science, we shall show that it is not contrary to our Scripture. But when they produce from any of their books a theory contrary to Scripture, and therefore contrary to the Catholic faith, either we shall have some ability to demonstrate that it is absolutely false, or at least we ourselves will hold it so without any shadow of a doubt.[15]

In this passage, Augustine distinguishes between scientific demonstration and scientific theory, a distinction that Galileo also makes.[16] A demonstration would involve a proof, such as would be found in the following syllogism,[17]

> All A are B.
> All B are C.
> Therefore, All A are C.

In a syllogism, if the form is valid and the premises are true, and the conclusion follows from the premises, then the conclusion *must* be true. So a demonstration would amount to a convincing argument as to the truth of a particular claim. Under the category of demonstration, Augustine would also include proofs derived from the experience of the natural world.[18] For example, Augustine writes with scorn about those who would argue that fish lack memory, because he had observed a group of fish that crowded around a particular place in a fountain after having been fed at that location.[19] Augustine would consider this experience to be proof of the fact that fish have memory, when taken in conjunction with similar experiences that had been documented by others.[20] It is on the basis of this demonstration that Augustine rejects the Scriptural interpretation of

---

15. Augustine, *De Genesi* I.21.41. See Galileo, "Letter," 194.
16. See Galileo, "Letter," 175.
17. Aristotle advocates this view in *Posterior Analytics* I.2,71b10–72b.
18. McMullen, "Galileo on Science and Scripture," 294.
19. Augustine, *De Genesi* III.8.12.
20. Ibid.

Genesis 1:24 that claims that "fish are not called 'living beings' but *creeping creatures having life* precisely because they have no memory."[21]

In contrast, a theory or hypothesis would be so-called because it lacks demonstration or proof.[22] For example, Augustine discusses two different theories with respect to the heavens; one that asserts the heavens are stationary and another that asserts that the heavens are moving.[23] He notes that there is no clear evidence demonstrating either theory and so he doesn't attempt to harmonize Scripture with either of them.[24] When a theory lacks demonstration, Scripture doesn't have to be harmonized with it. In fact, Augustine argues that if a scientific theory appears to be contrary to Scripture, then Christians are entitled to view that theory as false, even if the theory has not been falsified by a demonstration.[25]

Returning to the professors who defended geocentrism on the basis of a particular interpretation of Scripture, Augustine would argue that their interpretation could be falsified only by a scientific demonstration of heliocentrism. Since Copernicanism had not been demonstrated at the time Galileo wrote his *Letter*, Augustine would have identified it as a theory. Consequently, he would have argued that the Church was justified in holding her belief that the theory of Copernicanism was false, since it appeared to contradict her interpretation of Scripture. Furthermore, Augustine would have argued that the Church was not required to falsify Copernicanism before deeming it to be false, although he might have encouraged her to try to do so.

On this point, Galileo diverges from Augustine in order to defend Copernicanism, without explicitly stating that he is doing so. He argues that scientific theories should be falsified first, before they are condemned,

> Now if truly demonstrated physical conclusions need not be subordinated to biblical passages, but the latter must rather be shown not to interfere with the former, then before a physical proposition is condemned it must be shown to be not rigorously demonstrat-

21. Ibid. See also Genesis 1:24.

22. For an interesting discussion of the use of the term "hypothesis" in the time of Galileo, see Blackwell, *Galileo*, 80–81.

23. Augustine, *De Genesi* II.10.23.

24. Ibid.

25. Ibid., I.21.41.

ed—and this is to be done not by those who hold the proposition
to be true, but by those who judge it to be false.[26]

Galileo would argue that the Church was obligated to falsify
Copernicanism before she condemned it, not the heliocentrists. Augustine
would have argued that the Church was permitted to regard heliocentrism
as false since it lacked demonstration and since it appeared to conflict with
the established interpretation of particular Scriptural passages. In this case,
Galileo's argument would prove unsuccessful. Since the Church condemned
Copernicanism on the basis of an interpretation of Scripture *and* she held
absolute authority in matters of interpretation, she saw no need to engage
in the falsification of a heretical scientific theory. And Augustine, much to
Galileo's chagrin, would have agreed. Galileo's only recourse on this point
would be to follow Augustine's advice and to demonstrate Copernicanism.
In the face of such a demonstration, and according to Augustine's principle
of the harmonization of Scripture with demonstration, the Church would
have to reconsider her condemnation of Copernicanism.

Truth Is Unified

The third principle claims that truth is not self-contradictory. Hence, a
true scientific claim and an interpretation of Scripture, if true, cannot contradict one another. Both Augustine and Galileo presuppose that truth is
unified.[27] Truth does not contradict itself; truth contradicts falsehoods. If
a claim has been demonstrated to be true, then it cannot contradict what
has been correctly interpreted from Scripture. If there is a contradiction,
then either Scripture has been misinterpreted or there was not an actual
demonstration. Augustine offers the following example,

> Let us suppose that in explaining the words, *And God said, "Let
> there be light," and light was made,* one man thinks that it was
> material light that was made, and another that it was spiritual. As
> to the actual existence of spiritual light in a spiritual creature, our
> faith leaves no doubt; as to the existence of material light, celestial
> or supercelestial, even existing before the heavens, a light which
> could have been followed by night, there will be nothing in such a
> supposition contrary to the faith until unerring truth gives the lie

26. Galileo, "Letter," 194–95.

27. Augustine, *De Genesi* II.9.20. See also Galileo, "Letter," 186 and Blackwell,
Galileo, 76.

to it. And if that should happen, this teaching was never in Holy Scripture but was an opinion proposed by man in his ignorance. On the other hand, if reason should prove that this opinion is unquestionably true, it will still be uncertain whether this sense was intended by the sacred writer when he used the words quoted above, or whether he meant something else no less true.[28]

In this passage, Augustine assumes the unity of truth. Although Scriptural interpretations, if true, cannot contradict one another, Augustine notes that a given Scriptural passage could be interpreted in more than one sense. For example, he elects to interpret some of the verses in Genesis in both a historical and a figurative sense, as he explains,

> In all the sacred books, we should consider the eternal truths that are taught, the facts that are narrated, the future events that are predicted, and the precepts or counsels that are given. In the case of a narrative of events, the question arises as to whether everything must be taken in the figurative sense only, or whether it must be expounded and defended also as a faithful record of what happened. No Christian will dare say that the narrative must not be taken in a figurative sense. For St. Paul . . . explains the statement in Genesis, *And they shall be two in one flesh*, as a great mystery in reference to Christ and to the Church.[29]

Given that Augustine presupposes that Scripture can be interpreted in more than one sense, and that not every Scriptural interpretation expresses truth, there is some question as to how one assesses the truth of an interpretation. This question leads us to the next principle.

The Harmonization of Scriptural Interpretation with the Faith

The fourth principle of interpretation is the harmonization of Scriptural interpretation with the articles of faith. According to Augustine, Scriptural interpretation must be grounded "in the context of Scripture" and it must be "in harmony with our faith."[30] He identifies the Catholic faith with the beliefs articulated in the Apostles' Creed, although he would have to admit

---

28. Augustine, *De Genesi* I.19.38.

29. Ibid., I.1. Here, Augustine quotes St. Paul's interpretation of Gen 2:24 in Eph 5:32.

30. Ibid., I.21.41.

the future teachings of the Church Councils as providing an elaboration
and an extension of that faith,

> . . . we must first briefly explain the Catholic faith . . . Here is
> that faith: God the Father Almighty made and established all
> of creation through his only-begotten Son, that is, through the
> Wisdom and Power consubstantial and coeternal to himself, in the
> unity of the Holy Spirit, who is also consubstantial and coeternal.
> Therefore, the Catholic discipline commands that we believe that
> this Trinity is called one God and that he has made and created
> all the things that there are insofar as they are . . . Man, however,
> was renewed by Jesus Christ our Lord, when the ineffable and im-
> mutable Wisdom of God deigned to assume a whole and complete
> man and be born of the Holy Spirit and the Virgin Mary. He was
> crucified, buried, rose, and ascended into heaven—all of which has
> already happened. He is coming to judge the living and the dead
> at the end of the world and at the resurrection of the dead in the
> flesh—this is proclaimed as yet to come. The Holy Spirit was given
> to those who believe in him. He founded Mother Church which
> is called Catholic, because it is everywhere perfect, not at all weak,
> and because it is spread throughout the whole world. For those
> who do penance previous sins have been forgiven, and eternal life
> and the kingdom of heaven have been promised.[31]

Augustine assumes that both the context of the Scripture and the
articles of Christian faith provide a framework in which to interpret
Scripture and that interpretations can either be affirmed or rejected on the
basis of how they accord with this framework,

> When we read the inspired books in the light of this wide variety
> of true doctrines which are drawn from a few words and founded
> on the firm basis of Catholic belief, let us choose that one which
> appears as certainly the meaning intended by the author. But if
> this is not clear, then at least we should choose an interpretation
> in keeping with the context of Scripture and in harmony with our
> faith. But if the meaning cannot be studied and judged by the
> context of Scripture, at least we should choose only that which our
> faith demands. For it is one thing to fail to recognize the primary

---

31. St. Augustine, *On the Literal Interpretation of Genesis: An Unfinished Book*, trans.
Roland J. Teske, SJ (Washington, DC: The Catholic University of America Press, 1991)
1.2–4.

meaning of the writer, and another to depart from the norms of religious belief.[32]

Thus, all Scriptural interpretations must be consistent with the articles of Christian faith. With respect to the geocentrism of Galileo's enemies, there doesn't appear to be anything in geocentrism that would contradict the faith as articulated in the Creed. So an interpretation of Scripture in defence of geocentrism could not be ruled out on the basis of the Creed. However, the same could be said for an interpretation of Scripture in favour of Copernicanism.

The conflict between the Catholic faith and Copernicanism emerged because of a Church Council, namely, the fourth session of the Council of Trent (8 April 1546), which decreed that the Church was the final authority in matters of Scriptural interpretation. Since the Church had taken a geocentric position on the basis of Scripture, and since the Church was the authority with respect to preserving the Catholic faith, any scientific theory that contradicted her Scriptural interpretation could be condemned as heretical.

In order to address the Council of Trent, Galileo articulates the fifth interpretive principle, a principle that expresses support for Trent, when properly understood.

The Church is the Interpretive Authority in Matters of Faith and Practical Matters

The fifth interpretive principle is that the Church is the final authority on the interpretation of Scripture, with respect to matters of faith and practical matters. For this principle, Galileo cites the articles of the fourth session of the Council of Trent directly, which reads,

> To control petulant spirits, the Council decrees that, in matters of faith and morals, [including practical matters that extend beyond morals][33] pertaining to the edification of Christian doctrine, no one, relying on his own judgment and distorting the Sacred Scriptures according to his own conceptions, shall dare to interpret them contrary to that sense which Holy Mother Church, to whom it belongs to judge of their own true sense and meaning, has held

32. Augustine, *De Genesi* I.21.41.

33. See Blackwell's explanation of how "morals" extends beyond ethical matters, *Galileo*, 12–13.

and does hold, or even contrary to the unanimous agreement of the Fathers, even though such interpretations should never at any time be published. Those who do otherwise shall be identified by the ordinaries and punished in accordance with the penalties prescribed by the law.[34]

Galileo supported Trent, but argued that Copernicanism had nothing to do with matters of faith, Christian doctrine, or practice.[35] Hence, Trent should not have oversight with respect to the Copernican debate. It seems clear that Galileo's argument would not be a promising one, since the Church reserved the authority to decide for herself what matters counted as matters of faith, doctrine or practice. In particular, the Church took the position that her authority extended to matters implied by Scriptural interpretations, and thus Copernicanism was well within her purview.[36]

A stronger objection to Trent is found in Galileo's observation that the Church Fathers did not agree with respect to astronomy or the movement of the heavens, as Augustine pointed out.[37] Without consensus, there could be no official Patristic teaching on matters of astronomy, and thus Galileo would not be abrogating that aspect of Trent in supporting Copernicanism. However, Cardinal Bellarmine, the pre-eminent Catholic theologian of the day, disputed Galileo's observation, choosing rather to interpret Trent as indicating that certain eminent Fathers made authoritative judgments on some issues that were not contradicted by the other Fathers, rather than viewing Trent as an endorsement of unanimity amongst the Fathers.[38] Despite Galileo's arguments, Copernicanism was condemned in 1616 and Galileo was ordered to abandon Copernicanism personally by Cardinal Bellarmine.[39]

34. "Decrees of the Council of Trent Session IV: Decree on the Edition and on the Interpretation of the Sacred Scriptures." Trans. Richard J. Blackwell, in Blackwell, *Galileo*, 183.

35. Galileo, "Letter," 203.

36. Blackwell, *Galileo*, 19, 37–39.

37. Ibid., 202–4. See also Augustine, *De Genesi* II.10.23.

38. Blackwell, *Galileo*, 38.

39. Ibid., 125–27.

Conclusion

Galileo's use of Augustine in the *Letter* provides a theoretical structure in which new scientific theories, once demonstrated, can be compared with Scriptural interpretations and such interpretations can be re-interpreted if necessary in light of demonstration. Although the project of reconciling science and Scripture is challenging, his model provides a starting point for such a project. One of the interesting advantages to his view is that it encourages dialogue between scientists and theologians, with a view to reaching a common goal, truth. However, Galileo's model can only reconcile demonstrated scientific claims and interpretations of Scripture. But since Copernicanism was, as yet, undemonstrated, Galileo's model would not be useful in reconciling Copernicanism and Scripture at his moment of crisis. Nor is it clear how helpful Galileo's model would prove in a contemporary setting, in which science has largely abandoned a commitment to demonstration in favour of the pursuit of probability.

A further difficulty with Galileo's model becomes evident when one gives close attention to Augustine's writings. Galileo cites passages from Augustine in order to make several arguments, but he does not give sufficient attention to those aspects of Augustine's teachings concerning Scriptural interpretation that undermine Galileo's project, such as Augustine's commitment to the Catholic faith, which I am convinced would have extended to the Church Councils. So although his usage of Augustine is helpful in his escape from excommunication, Augustine would not have agreed with Galileo's opinion that it was the responsibility of the Church to falsify Copernicanism.

In conclusion, let me say a few words about Galileo's confidence in science. Although Galileo is optimistic about the power of human reason and the role of demonstration, he is aware of the fact that human reason has its limitations,

> I have no doubt that where human reasoning cannot reach—and where consequently we can have no science but only opinion and faith—it is necessary in piety to comply absolutely with the strict sense of Scripture.[40]

According to Galileo, reason is not to be substituted for faith. It is to coexist with faith, continuing where human reason cannot reach.

40. Ibid., 197.

However, no one should prevent human reasoning from attempting to discover things about God's creation or to attempt to reach the threshold of its rational ability. As a general principle, this is something that Augustine would have endorsed whole-heartedly and that perhaps might form the beginning of a new dialogue between science and Christianity.[41]

41. Thanks to the participants in "Figured Out," a conference held at Tyndale University College in May of 2006 for their helpful comments on a previous version of this paper. Special thanks are also extended to La Fondation Hardt in Vandoeuvres, Switzerland, for allowing me to be a Visiting Researcher in the summer of 2006, during which I undertook the revisions of this paper.

Afterword

The first Tyndale Conference on Biblical Interpretation was in May, 2006, and the present volume grows out of it; its theme was "figuration in biblical interpretation." In the reformation now taking place within professional biblical studies, figuration is one of the most exciting developments, and it arises directly out of the urgency of acknowledging the Bible as scripture and of reading it theologically.

Tyndale University College is an undergraduate faculty, primarily in the liberal arts, and its disciplinary breadth made it natural to sponsor such a conference. That breadth is visible in essays in this volume from its members in history, literature, and philosophy, as well as in theology and Bible. The conference received strong and faithful support from Tyndale's Provost, Dr. Earl Davey, and from the Academic Dean of the University College, Dr. Dan Scott. Jennifer Hart Weed gave continuing and valuable leadership as co-chair of the planning committee..

Chris Seitz and Ephraim Radner were our keynote speakers, and we thank Chris for allowing us to use the title of his book, *Figured Out*, as the title of our conference, and for contributing to this volume through his essay on historicism and figuration. And we also thank Keith Bodner for letting us use the title of his paper for our own volume. Ephraim Radner's paper, "Leviticus as Christian Scripture," contains material that subsequently appeared in his commentary on Leviticus in the Brazos series, and appears here by permission.

To bring this volume up to small-book size, we've added three papers that were not read at the conference, and thank our friends Nathan MacDonald and Frank Spina for sharing with us some of their figuration.

Finally, and above all, we praise God for the gift of the Word—living, written, and preached—as we ever seek from the inspiring Spirit the light to understand it, the grace to obey it, and the power to proclaim it.

Stanley D. Walters

Select Bibliography

Bodner, Keith. *David Observed: A King in the Eyes of His Court.* Hebrew Bible Monographs 5. Sheffield: Sheffield Phoenix, 2005.

Childs, Brevard S. *Introduction to the Old Testament as Scripture.* Philadelphia: Fortress, 1979.

———. *The Struggle to Understand Isaiah as Christian Scripture.* Grand Rapids: Eerdmans, 2004.

Collins, John J., and Craig A. Evans, editors. *Christian Beginnings and the Dead Sea Scrolls,* Acadia Studies in Bible and Theology. Grand Rapids: Baker Academic, 2006.

Davis, Ellen. *Wondrous Depth: Preaching the Old Testament* (Louisville: Westminster John Knox, 2005.

Fishbane, Michael. *Garments of Torah: Essays in Biblical Hermeneutics.* Indiana Studies in Biblical Literature. Bloomington: Indiana University Press, 1989.

Frei, Hans W. *The Eclipse of Biblical Narrative: A Study in Eighteenth and Nineteenth Century Hermeneutics.* New Haven: Yale University Press, 1974.

Greene-McCreight, Kathryn. *Ad Litteram: How Augustine, Calvin and Barth Read the "Plain Sense" of Genesis 1–3.* Issues in Systematic Theology 5. New York: Lang, 1999.

Lioy, Dan. *The Search for Ultimate Reality: Intertextuality between the Genesis and Johannine Prologues.* Studies in Biblical Literature 93. New York: Lang, 2005.

Rad, Gerhard von. "Typological Interpretation of the Old Testament." In *Essays on Old Testament Hermeneutics,* edited by Claus Westermann, 17–39. Translated by James Luther Mays. Atlanta: John Knox, 1963.

Radner, Ephraim. *Hope among the Fragments: The Broken Church and Its Engagement of Scripture.* Grand Rapids: Brazos, 2004.

———. "Sublimity and Providence: The Spiritual Discipline of Figural Reading." *Ex Auditu* 18 (2002) 155–70.

———, and George Sumner, editors. *The Rule of Faith: Scripture, Canon, and Creed in a Critical Age.* Harrisburg, PA: Morehouse, 1998.

Rosenberg, Joel. *King and Kin: Political Allegory in the Hebrew Bible.* Indiana Studies in Biblical Literature. Bloomington: Indiana University Press, 1986.

Seitz, Christopher R. *Figured Out: Typology and Providence in Christian Scripture.* Louisville: Westminster John Knox, 2001.

———. *Prophecy and Hermeneutics: Toward a New Introduction to the Prophets.* Studies in Theological Interpretation. Grand Rapids: Baker Academic, 2007.

———. *Word without End: The Old Testament as Abiding Theological Witness.* Grand Rapids: Eerdmans, 1998.

————, and Kathryn Greene-McCreight, editors. *Theological Exegesis: Essays in Honor of Brevard S. Childs.* Grand Rapids: Eerdmans, 1999.

Walters, Stanley D. "The Needy is King: Preaching with a Contextual Hermeneutic." *Toronto Journal of Theology* 5 (1989) 88–103.

————. "Reading Samuel to Hear God." *Calvin Theological Journal* 37 (2002) 61–81.

————. "The Voice of God's People in Exile." *Ex Auditu* 10 (1994) 73–86.

Watts, Rikki. *Isaiah's New Exodus in Mark.* Biblical Studies Library. Grand Rapids: Baker, 2000.

Made in the USA
Middletown, DE
12 July 2022

69131406R00097